BHANGRA

Bhangra

Birmingham and beyond

Dr Rajinder Dudrah

with contributions from Boy Chana & Ammo Talwar

Published in September 2007 by
Birmingham City Council Library & Archive Service
© Text copyright 2007: Dr Rajinder Dudrah
© Publishing rights 2007: Birmingham City Council
Library & Archive Service

ISBN 0-7093-0256-8

Written by Dr Rajinder Dudrah
Designed by Bharat Patel
Printed in England by Renfor Four Colour Ltd

Punch
Studio 112/113, The Greenhouse
Gibb Street, Birmingham B9 4AA
T: +44 (0)121 224 7444
F: +44 (0)121 224 7441
E: info@punch-records.co.uk
www.sohoroadtothepunjab.org
www.punch-records.co.uk

Punch gratefully acknowledges financial assistance
from Heritage Lottery Fund and Birmingham City Council.

Inside cover photo: Jaysons, Soho Road, Birmingham
© Ian Reynolds, www.i4images.com.
pp.2–3: Heera live at The Dome, Birmingham, 1987.
pp.4–5: The Punjab Dancers (stationery detail), 1973.

Photo credits: pp.8, 9, 10, 25, 30, 50, 56, 63, 65, 70, 77 (Punjab Lane)
© Ian Reynolds, www.i4images.com; p.71 © BBC Archives; pp.2, 60,
67, 74, 75, 76: courtesy of Boy Chana; pp.6, 29, 34, 35, 52: courtesy of
Kalayan; pp.15, 23, 26, 87: courtesy of Kash Sahota; p.20: courtesy of
Mangal Singh; p.59: courtesy of Hard Kaur; p.72: courtesy of Nachural
Records; p.77 (Panjabi MC): courtesy of PMC Records.

Contents

Acknowledgements

Rajinder, Gursharan (Boy Chana), and Ammo wish to thank the following individuals and organisations for their interest, enthusiasm and support during the preparation of this book: Birmingham Library and Archive Services, Birmingham, UK, and the Heritage Lottery Fund, for funding this publication, and for the archiving and care of the Bhangra Collection of written, published and photographic source material, memorabilia and ephemera, collected by the author and contributors during the course of research for this work and deposited at Birmingham Central Library.

Rajinder would like to thank: Ammo for his creative and organisational vision and 'let's do it' attitude, despite being frenetically busy almost all the time. To all the Bhangra artists and audiences, old and new, thanks for keeping the music and culture alive and kicking, and a special appreciation to the artists and music aficionados who gave up their time for the interviews used in the publication. Thanks to all the staff at Punch Records for their consistent work behind the scenes – keep up the good work Punch! I am grateful to Malcolm Dick for offering comments on an earlier draft of Chapters 4 and 5, to Helen O'Brien and Gerry Box for offering comments on Chapter 3, and to Gerry Box (thanks again) for her proof reading of the manuscript. Bharat – top man for the design work, cheers! Mandeep Malhi – a cheerful spirit with a good eye for design detail. Richard Albutt – thank you for your digitisation work and support throughout the project. A good shout out to Simon Redgrave for his commitment and energy behind the *Soho Road to the Punjab* exhibition. A big 'Kiddha Shera' to my friend Ashok Mahay (Shorki) for DJing with me in his multi-coloured sequined top on 4 December 1987 at the Bhangra dance competition at Aston Manor School (I was wearing a pink bow tie, no less!). To my family (Mum, Dad, brothers and sisters, including my nieces and nephews) and friend Lloyd Williams, who supported me during isolated periods of research and writing this book – this is for all of you: 'Balle, Balle, Shava, Shava' (Bravo, Bravo!). I would like to dedicate this book to my sister Harjinder Rall (Pinky) who was my friend, collaborator and anchor of support at secondary school, not least when we used to organise Bhangra dance events together in the mid-to-late 80s.

Mohinder Kaur's music workshop, late 1960s.

Gursharan would like to add: The internet is a wonderful tool, but the best knowledge is gained from the written word and in books you can feel – and you get to keep them for generations. This is one of the reasons why I wanted to be part of this book; one that charts aspects of the life of Punjabis who have made something from a life in post-industrial Britain; it is in many ways about you all. I would like to thank Ammo for sharing the same vision and pulling together a great team of people. Without him my vision would still be in cardboard boxes. Rajinder – you are an inspirational, motivating person and writer and I am happy that you were chosen to be the editor. Gurcharan Mall – respect is due to a true pioneer of UK Bhangra music and culture. Personally, I thank my parents – late Mr Harkewal Singh Chana (Baddon-Hoshiarpur) and Mrs Kuldip Kaur Chana. My wife Brinda for giving me the time and love to make an ambition come true. My children, Sharnita and Aaron – my love is all around you, you make us proud of what you do. My family Satbinder and Debbie, Manmohan and Jasbinder, Jasbinder and Karamjit, Taranjit, late Gurshanpal Kaur Chana, Jaspal and Tony Seerha. My nephews and nieces – Arjan, Sarah, Rachel, Roshan, Aman, Rajdeep and Inderdeep Chana, and Jeevan Seerha. Mr Malkit Chand and Mrs Mindo Chand and family, and the Rattu family – thanks for all the help in babysitting and support. T L Roadshow – probably the finest roadshow in Birmingham: Bobby, John, Rax and roadies through the years 1989–2003, etc. Hans, Prem, Raj, Munesh, Harpreet (money-spinner) and thanks to Anari Sangeet Party for the early sound systems. Iqbal Nandra for giving me the contact for *Eastern Eye* – Sarwar Ahmed and the original *Eastern Eye* music team: Kam Kaur, Puneet Chahal, Suky Bhamra, and Venno Deewan (GB).

A big thanks to all those who feature in the book. Those who we have missed, please don't be mad just think about getting even with your own book! Enjoy the fact that we have all in one way or another made history and have a legacy to be proud of.

Ammo wishes to acknowledge: Without the art we have no book so my first thanks will be to the early influencers, party rockers and stalwarts of this multi-million pound industry – you know who you are! Ultimately you have all somehow affected our practise and guided our vision. I would personally like unconditionally to thank my mentors, supporters and family who continually help to shape my life. Thanks to Mom and Dad, Suki Talwar, Pina Talwar and Amanda Talwar, Rajinder Dudrah, Boy Chana, Simon Redgrave, Bharat 'Secret Bhangramuffin' Patel, Brigitte Windsor, Richard Albutt, Mandeep Mahli, Sunder Singh and Ian Reynolds; the Bhangra champions for the exhibition including San-j Sanj, Sheni, Kalayan and Kash; Heritage Lottery Fund in particular Katie Foster and Sita Ramamurthy; Punch crew including Cynthia Torto, Josie Davies and Mary Wakeman; and finally all the international DJs, media partners and artists that make the industry tick. Chak De Phattey!

MAXIMUM RESPECT

SAINT

RECORDS

CHALLA

1992

B

STEREO

45 rpm

MSCSR 007

Foreword

EVER SINCE I STARTED COLLECTING RECORDS I was always a stickler for reading sleeve notes. My obsession for information coupled with my localised politics living in 80's Birmingham raised many questions around British Asian music – its written text, archived information and learning resources. Two very different stalwarts of the scene have really pushed the boundaries of text and image to create this publication (Rajinder Dudrah, academic and cultural commentator, and Boy Chana, photographer and journalist) and I feel honoured to be part of the project.

AS BIRMINGHAM heads towards 2012 as the UK's first majority non-white city, subcultures, cultural values, understandings of displaced communities and general 'fight the power' mentality become ever more important. THE WORD 'BHANGRA' evokes many thoughts, memories, feelings and emotions – from the singing, dancing and joyous celebrations of Vaisakhi, the daytime warehouse parties in the late 80s, the chart-topping sound of Panjabi MC, right through to American R'n'B and Hip-Hop artists moving away from sampling Funk & Jazz, to sampling Asian sounds (e.g. Missy Elliot's 'Get Ur Freak On' in 2001).

Bhangra has echoes similar to other displaced musical movements such as Jazz in New Orleans, House in Chicago, Techno in Detroit, Northern Soul in Wigan and Dance music throughout the warehouse scene in the UK. DJs and sound system networks operated amongst a community thrown up in a whirlwind during Thatcher's reign in the 1980s. Bhangra, in its traditional sense, creates a soundscape of celebration of the harvest but in post-war Britain it had metamorphosized.

The songs and music had shifted from joyous harvest celebrations to working class drama, theatricality and performance with a strong sense of 1980's doom and gloom. Dub Bhangra poetry interposed with a new wave of folklore tales with a spiritual and religious twist, elevating pioneering groups like Bhujhangy and Anari Sangeet into the limelight. Cultural networks were growing, bands were developing larger sounds with stereo influences coupled with an increasing financial infrastructure, and new labels were emerging – the artists were beginning to understand the business of the music industry.

'Fusion' and 'mainstream' were always words that were synonymous with the 1980s British Bhangra industry – attempts were being made at 'crossing over'. Roadshows assisted in pushing the Asian sound system into the limelight. New Brit-Asian entrepreneurs emerged in this scene and became the voice of the youth, fusing British Asian popular culture within a time span

that was probably the most vibrant period of the UK's music industry – if only it had fully realised it.

Elements of Rave culture alongside the Soul/Jazz movement were interplayed alongside Hip-Hop, New Jack Swing juxtaposed alongside hard-hitting Bhangra beats mixed in with Detroit Techno – all the BPM's (beats per minute) seemed to mix in seamlessly; jumping from clubs on a weekday to weddings on the weekends. The early folk Bhangra music pioneered by artists like Chamkila, Jamla Jat, Kuldip Manak, Gurdas Maan, Narinder Biba, Parkash Kaur and others, was given an eclectic fusion, articulated with a distinctive UK sound through bands like Alaap, Apna Sangeet, Azaad, Chirag Pehchan, DCS, Heera, Holle Holle, Premi, and The Sahotas.

Birmingham was instrumental in this shift and is the starting point of this book. I'm sure in years to come the Bhangra legacy will once again metamorphosize into other new genres, and while new forms of music 'come and go', Bhangra has proved it is here to stay.

'Chak De Phattey!' (Lift the floorboards/ Mash-up the dance floor!)

Amarjit 'Ammo' Talwar
Director of Punch
2007

Introduction: Drum 'n' Dhol

Rajinder Dudrah

Glad rags abound, boys looking sharp and girls sharper still. Vibrant colours and *desi* (diasporic South Asian) dress styles coalesce with the best of Western haute couture. A live band plays the Indian drums – the *dhol*, tablas and *dholaks* – alongside a drum kit, keyboards, and bass and electric guitars, with a lead singer at the microphone. A DJ set adorns the stage, throwing in live mixing and MCing for good measure, chatting in Punjabi and Jamaican patois over breakbeats of Hip-Hop, Garage and Grime. The lyrics of the songs, both from the band and over the DJ's decks, range from a love story about two teenagers, to the travails of migration to the inner cities. The DJ sends a shout out 'To the Birmingham massive!'.

The crowd becomes ecstatic and dances with extra glee, their bodies moving in ways that are part South Asian, part Western, and more besides. This is a British Bhangra night in the city of Birmingham, UK.

Scenes like these have justified Birmingham's status as capital of contemporary British Bhangra music. Over the last 20-plus years, the city has been home to some of the genre's biggest names (**Achanak, Anari Sangeet Party, Apna Group, A.S. Kang, B21, Bally Jagpal, Bhujhangy, Balbir and Dalbir Khanpur, DCS, Dr Zeus, Dalvinder Singh, Jazzy B, Jassi Sidhu, Hard Kaur, Malkit Singh, Mesophuria, Nachda Hasdey, Safri Boyz, Sukshinder Shinda, The Dhol Blasters,**

XLNC...). Birmingham houses key record labels, studios and distribution companies, responsible for the steady production of new albums over the last two decades (**Oriental Star Agency** on Moseley Road, **Nachural Records** in Smethwick, **Envy Roma Music** in Handsworth, **Moviebox Records** in Small Heath). This collection of musical talent and expertise, coupled with a culture of live performances at student gigs and private celebratory parties, and a growing DJ culture, makes Birmingham an important centre of the British Bhangra music industry.

As music for South Asians in Britain, Bhangra dates from the late 1960s and follows the post-war arrival of migrant workers from the Indian subcontinent

Bhangra Time, vol.2:
Rani Soho Road Dee
(cover detail),
Oriental Star.

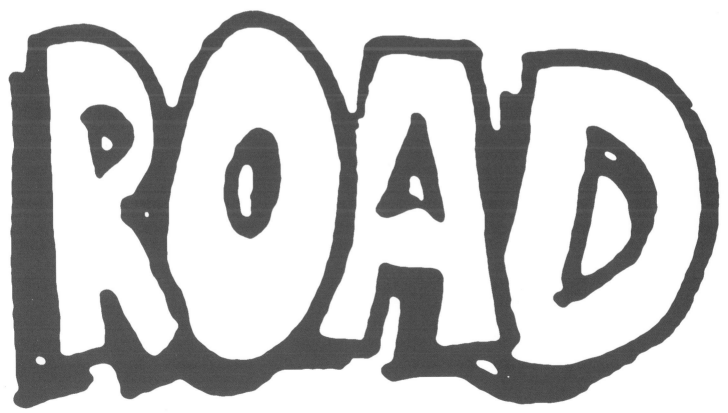

and East Africa. Many settled in the West Midlands, importing records alongside early Indian film music. One of the most popular genres was Bhangra, sung in Punjabi. This traditional folk music is performed on festival occasions as a song and dance, and is always accompanied by at least one *dhol* (a large, double-sided cylindrical drum). An *alghoza* (a twin flute) may also accompany the singing and dancing party, which consists mostly of male members. As they dance, the performers take turns singing, with the lyrics generally heroic in tone, often in praise of the motherland. These features fed the nostalgia of first generation South Asians in their new British surroundings, where they could reminisce about their cultures and countries of origin, especially in the context of their grim employment and housing conditions, and their encounters with racism from sections of white British society.

A distinctively British Bhangra took shape in the mid-1980s as an emerging second generation of South Asian musicians began to experiment and improvise with technology, marking a direct engagement with notions of British and Asian identity by locating their music in a British Asian experience. For example, the 1988 song *Soho Road Uteh* (On Soho Road) by the Birmingham band **Apna Sangeet** (Our Music) was immensely popular for referencing the recognisable. It describes a story in which two lovers meet in India, become separated and then attempt to find each other through a 'love quest-

cum-song as journey'. Among the places travelled and searched we hear of Bradford, Coventry, Derby, London, and Soho Road in Handsworth. Interestingly, all these areas are inscribed with their South Asian settlements as politicised movements. 'Soho Road' has global resonance for young Asians well beyond Birmingham, and is often deployed in British Bhangra tracks. It invokes an easily identifiable social, cultural and political space made and developed by British South Asians and other migrant groups; an iconic reference point.

With Bhangra's popularity spreading amongst many South Asian youth across the country, by the late 1980s some bands attempted to crossover into the mainstream charts, including Birmingham's DCS with their 1991 track *Rule Britannia* (see Chapter 3).

British Bhangra can be characterised as an urban anthem for many British South Asians, incorporating their pleasures, pains and politics. For British Bhangra artists and their audiences, the songs and music are as quintessentially British as Balti curries or the Royal Family. As a case in point, the Birmingham-based British Bhangra band **Achanak** (literally translated as 'suddenly', referring to the band's rapid emergence on the British Bhangra scene in the late 80s with the track *Lak Noo Halade* – Move That Hip) continually used the word 'Nach' in all or part of the titles to their albums of the 90s: *NACHurally*, *paNACHe*, *sigNACHure*, *sNACH*, and *Top NACH*. 'Nach' means 'dance' and the clever play and combination

Poster advertising a local Bhangra radio show, corner of Soho Road, Handsworth, 1999.

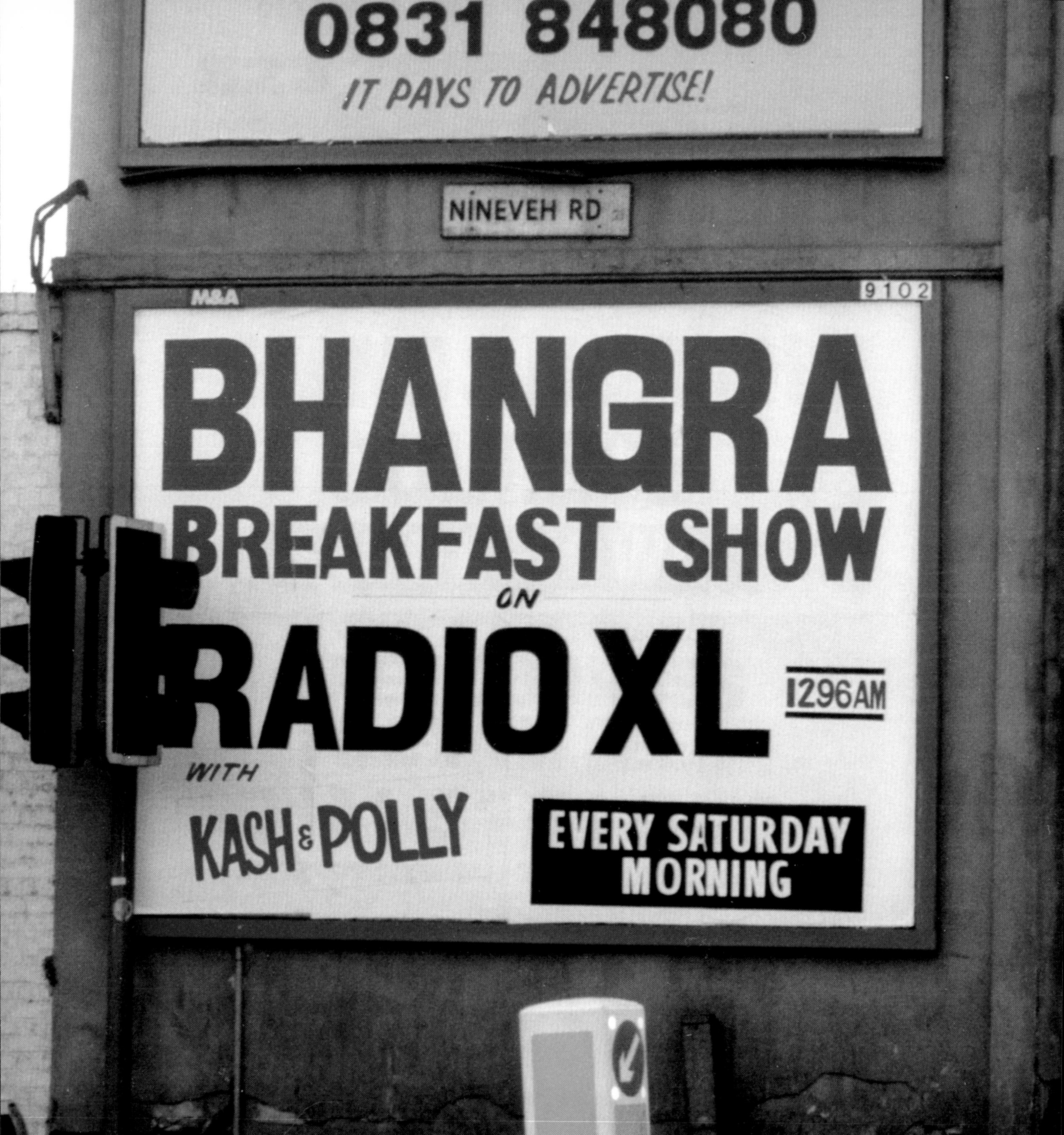

0831 848080
IT PAYS TO ADVERTISE!
NINEVEH RD
M&A
9102
BHANGRA
BREAKFAST SHOW
ON
RADIO XL
1296AM
WITH
KASH & POLLY
EVERY SATURDAY
MORNING

of this Hindi/Punjabi/Urdu meaning
with a vernacular British vocabulary
illustrates the band's eclectic vision
for British popular music and its
ensuing identities.

Beyond Birmingham
This book is designed to offer a timely
and accessible overview of some of
the artists, events, songs, audiences,
and images of British Bhangra music,
from its folk derivations to a diversified
music industry that now encompasses a
range of fusion-based British Asian genres. The
city of Birmingham is the starting point to the
narrative of this publication, particularly, given
its importance to the British Bhangra music
industry, but it is only one co-ordinate on the
map of UK-based Bhangra. Through the chapters
that follow, other cities and places are also registered
as playing their part in the ongoing story of British
Bhangra (for example, London and Coventry). The book
uses both textual analysis and interviews. Textual analysis,
to offer close readings about some of the songs, lyrics and
images (most notably of album sleeves) in British Bhangra.
Interviews with artists, lyricists, musicians and DJs feature
throughout the publication. The interviewees are introduced as they
appear in the book. The interview extracts are used to illustrate
an overview of the musical genre as it has developed in post-

Soho Road has global resonance for young Asians well beyond Birmingham, and is often deployed in British Bhangra tracks. It invokes an easily identifiable social, cultural and political space made and developed by British South Asians and other migrant groups; an iconic reference point.

war Britain from its early folk Bhangra days to a fully fledged music industry that is increasingly making in-roads into mainstream Western culture and society. Two sets of interviews have been used. One that was conducted during the spring and summer months of 2007 with key Bhangra music practitioners, and the other that is drawn from a PhD study by the lead author (Dudrah 2001). This latter set of interviews is indicated in the main text of the book via footnotes which source the doctorate study.

Keywords
It is worth outlining here a few of the keywords that appear throughout the book as it illustrates its account of British Bhangra.

The British Bhangra music industry
Since its emergence in the late 60s, Bhangra music in Britain has consisted of and brought together hundreds of people (British South Asian and others) throughout the UK and beyond; including singers, musicians, technicians and those involved in the record companies. This sizable space for British South Asian cultural production and its related economies warrants its recognition

as an industry. This includes the: economies related to the buying and selling of music and recording equipment; technological expertise; production, marketing and selling of music tapes, records and compact discs; the production of music videos; music sale returns for the investment of future projects and work; performance of live music and DJs at gigs; and websites on the internet. Also, artists involved in Bhangra's production and distribution, as well as DJs regularly playing the music over the radio airwaves, and music writers in the British South Asian popular press, describe the collaborative music scene as such.[1]

Old Skool Bhangra
From the late 60s onwards, the beginnings of Bhangra music listening, performing and recording began in Britain. By the mid-80s and into the early 90s, the 'heyday' of live and recorded British Bhangra music was in motion. Predominantly young men in their late teens to early 30s were getting together through networks of friendship, locality, and kith and kin, to form different Bhangra groups, responding to the musical demands of a growing British South Asian youth culture. The heyday sound drew

Golden Star (UK), *Hey! Jamalo Def Mix*, remixed by Bally Sagoo (cover detail), Oriental Star, 1990.

heavily on the early folk Bhangra influences and articulated them alongside a range of genres from across the globe: Western Pop, Disco, Reggae, Rock, R'n'B, Hip-Hop, Ragga, Hindi film music, *Qawallis*, etc. The reference to 'Old Skool Bhangra' throughout this publication acknowledges this period of music-making in British Bhangra's history.

Post-Bhangra

The term 'post-Bhangra' references music that owes a debt of gratitude to both folk Punjabi music and Old Skool Bhangra, either through the use of their beats, music and/or lyrics. This music is increasingly fusion-based and draws on the latest computer software technologies to produce contemporary sounds. Live bands are increasingly less important in the production and performance of this genre of music, and DJs and music producers are equally considered artists like the singers, and state of the art PA (public address) systems feature heavily. The term 'post-' marks the arrival of this eclectic music as superseding the heyday of Old Skool Bhangra. Examples of post-Bhangra artists and music (e.g. Rishi Rich) are mentioned throughout the book.

Chapter 1 recounts aspects of the heyday of Bhangra music production through an interview with the songwriter Dr Bal Sidhu, paying attention to the role and importance of the lyrics. Chapter 2 charts the arrival of the live music scene during Bhangra's heyday and credits the role of concert promoters (through an interview with Gurd Chahal), who were key players in organising such live events. Chapter 3 offers a close textual reading of some album sleeve covers, examining the visual iconography that accompanied the music and lyrics. Chapter 4 provides a critical account of the mainstream white media reportage of Old Skool Bhangra; as British Bhangra became more noticeable in the larger urban British cities it attracted varied media attention. Chapter 5 places the account of women in Bhangra as equally important to that of the work of male artists. The stories, experiences and musical productions of some female artists are accounted for. In Chapter 6 Gursharan Chana offers a personal account of the rise and importance of the British Asian DJ in the story of British Bhangra music. Chapter 7 offers an account of the state of British Bhangra in the contemporary moment, looking back at developments in the music industry and the new challenges it faces in the 21st century.

This book is not intended as an authoritative or fixed account of the story of British Bhangra music. Rather it is offered as one narrative, from the vantage point of British Bhangra in Birmingham and wider afield, that has been selectively and sincerely ordered by its writing collaborators (Rajinder Dudrah, Gursharan Chana and Ammo Talwar). Its overall aim is to provide a starting point for its readers to offer other stories of and within the genre of the music, and to continue to chronicle the ongoing developments of British Bhangra.

1 For a more detailed account of the British
   Bhangra industry see Dudrah 2002.

1 Old Skool Bhangra

Boy Chana and Rajinder Dudrah

Chirag Pehchan, *Rail Gaddi (The Train)*, 1987.
Below: Chirag Pehchan, Asian Live Aid, 1985.

The lyricist is a key artist in the composition of Bhangra music as it is often they who draw on source material for the contents of the lyrics. These often shift between the cultures of the homeland (Punjab, India) and the new cultures in Britain. The contexts for producing some Old Skool Bhangra lyrics are illustrated here in an interview with Dr Bal Sidhu (also affectionately known as 'Sidhu bhetan-wala – writer of songs'), a formidable lyricist of British Bhangra since the 1970s. Dr Sidhu has penned some of the most popular songs to date – in some cases literally on his prescription sheets in his spare moments while working as a General Practitioner!

Dr Sidhu was brought up in the Midlands, studied medicine at University in Wales and is now settled in Coventry. His involvement in the British Bhangra music industry, initially as a part-time hobby, has given him a sense of belonging to a wider entertainment community in addition to his business enterprises:

I was brought up in West Bromwich, trained in Cardiff; went to Dudley, Birmingham, London as a medical registrar – all over the place – and then eventually back in '86 I settled in Coventry as a GP…I went into the business of nursing homes, then properties and now we are doing projects all over the world with Jindy Khaira from KTC Foods. So I have spent most of my life in the business of medicine and housing. I enjoy medicine, I've got my own practice…music was always a hobby, but it gave me a circle of friends in the musical world in the entertainment industry, which I really look up to…the music industry, the media gave me a circle. Like you have a family circle, like you have a business circle – in the nursing homes, the hotels, the properties, the medical circle…so it's given me yet another circle, which brings excitement to your everyday living, and that's something I look out for – the next big lyric to excite me.

As a teenager, studying at college and then university, Bal Sidhu was influenced by the early bands and artists in the Midlands of the 1970s: **Anari Sangeet Party**, **A.S. Kang** and **Bhujhangy Group**. **Jandu Litteranwala**, one of the early lyricists of the 70s was also an inspiration, especially in his collaborations on song lyrics for the artist A.S. Kang. Litteranwala drew on Punjabi culture and folklore which was transformed in post-war Britain. Bal Sidhu followed in this tradition of writing lyrics, blending South Asian and British lives that people were living at home, college and work in the 70s and 80s.

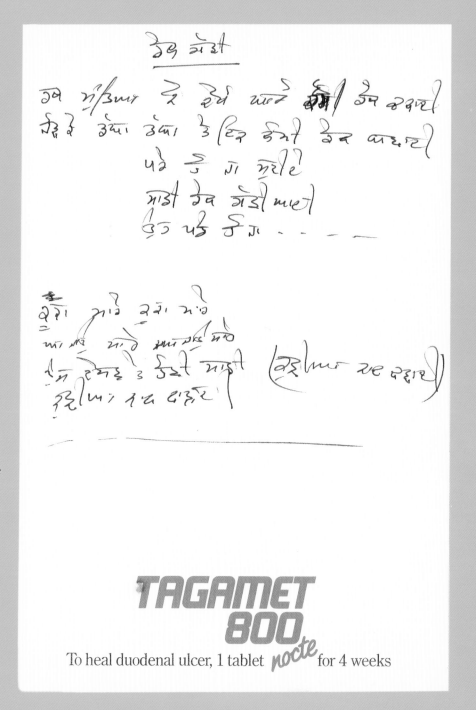

Dr Sidhu's original lyrics to *Rail Gaddi*.

Anari Sangeet Party, *Best of Anari Sangeet Party*, Oriental Star. Below: A.S. Kang, *Jawani* (cover detail), Roma, 1995.

Drawing from Punjabi culture, Dr Sidhu wrote wedding poems that were sung or recited to wish the bride, groom and their families well, during this act of union. For Dr Sidhu the wedding lyrics were important in engaging with his audiences through an emotional response:

...the encouragement I was given from the elders as a young student was great and I particularly valued my sera sikhia. This was a wedding poem and by looking at the number of ladies crying and then the joy in their eyes it had to be emotionally touching. You're saying something and it's touching them and that's what a song is all about. A song is your emotions which you're translating to words and then people listen to words and then it gets transferred back to emotions. So its emotions, words, then back to emotions.

Bal wrote his first song for Bhujhangy Group from Birmingham – entitled *25, 36, 25, 36* – a hybrid use of English and Punjabi that was about the ideal figure of a beautiful woman.
Dr Sidhu continued with this mix in his lyrics, giving inspiration and ideas to Bhangra singers and musicians to further blend Anglo-Indian lyrics with their fusion-based music and beats.
The idea behind one of Sidhu's most famous Bhangra tracks, *Rail Gaddi*

(The Train, 1987), comes from bringing together global, Western and Indian ideas. As he puts it:

...that sort of encourages you to think logically and to come up with ideas, and this is where the song *Rail Gaddi* came from, because in medical school days there are English parties, and it's always a traditional thing where people will go in a line and do a Conga dance. And I always used to think we don't have anything where we can create unity at happy times. Then I had to use a symbol to make this happen. You could use train, a snake...and then it sort of clicked one day that for Punjabi people the train is the right symbol, industrious and a link to communities. Having written it, it was more difficult to persuade people like Mangal Singh to sing it.

The song became a huge hit for the band Chirag Pehchan who released an album of

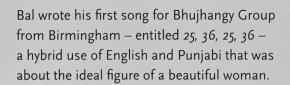

the same name in 1987, and was sung by their lead singer Mangal Singh. Such is its popularity, the song is still requested at parties and friends and families form long lines dancing out this hybrid Conga! The success of this track moved Bal Sidhu into the limelight as a creative lyricist who became sought after by numerous bands, particularly the Bhangra bands that were emerging during the mid-to-late 80s:

> ...before *Rail Gaddi* time I used to write a lot of songs and carry them around and see if somebody would sing them, but when it became such a big hit everybody was saying whatever I've got lets record it. It was the young bands like **Anaamika**, **Pardesi Music Machine**, **Balwinder Safri** and then **Malkit Singh** who all came around to record random songs I had written. And then, when we had disasters like the Indian earthquake, record companies and producers came to me to write a storyboard song and *Aftershock* came along.

Dr Sidhu's fame as a lyricist also introduced him to a sense of social responsibility, and the power that Bhangra music could generate as a medium for communication with second and third generation British Asian youth. Alongside his lyrics that were more celebratory or boisterous in tone, he began to cover a wider range of themes in response to world events – the plight of earthquake victims in India, and youth issues such as drug abuse:

Dr Bal Sidhu, songwriter.
Below: Malkit Singh (left) and his brother Harvinder Singh.

> Then all these bands started pushing me to do special songs and I was approached by Bradford City Council to write a song about saying no to drugs. The youngsters like to listen to these Bhangra artists and sort of listen more...to them, to say it's not good for them to have drugs or

23

Pardesi, *Pump Up The Bhangra* (cover detail), Oriental Star, 1988.

to smoke. They approached me and paid me to organise the singers ... and the recording session ... then we were approached by the BBC Asian Programmes Unit who took on the initiative of *Aftershock* and they did a video of it and approached writers in Mumbai to write their version, and I wrote the UK version.

This encouraged Bal to reflect on his practice as a lyricist who, for him, always needs to keep his creative mind open to how he is influenced by other co-artists, while also being aware of his own skills and abilities. Dr Sidhu acknowledged the input and work of other lyricists of British Bhangra who have helped to produce some memorable songs:

> Jandu Litteranwala is still writing for the big names like **Malkit Singh** and **Jazzy B**. There is a difference in the way Jandu and I would treat a topic. There's a difference of the language you use, there's a difference of the terminology you use. There's a weighing of the word that is different and the terminology should come out, otherwise it doesn't make any sense. You see the writer's life is different. A writer's life is a very long spell. [At any one time] ... you could be listening to a song written by Jandu, Dayalpuri, Chaman Lal Chaman, or me.

More recently, as Bal Sidhu is increasingly working across his full-time professional careers, writing lyrics has become less regular, though no less passionate. He is still approached by some of the newer artists who are fusing Old Skool Bhangra beats with emerging international musical sounds – following in the footsteps of the pioneers of the 80s, like **Kuljit Bhamra**. Although cautious, he is hopeful that the new trend in Bhangra and post-Bhangra music will try and emulate the excitement and emotion of Old Skool Bhangra; as live acts are increasingly giving way to lip-synching on stage, or at best PA systems do away with the need for live musicians:

Nowadays I don't write songs and keep them in my pocket. I have an idea and I keep it with me and when an artist usually rings me from the studio, or they come here, they say they are recording today or day after, I say fine I'll do one now, when everything is ready to go and it's fresh. I have recently written a track for **Juggy D** where **Rishi Rich** is doing the music. They gave me the idea, and within about 25 minutes I had written the song for them. Rishi Rich is doing exactly what Kuljit Bhamra was doing in the 80s and he has the same enthusiastic singers like Mangal Singh. It's really exciting. I just hope that all the new singers can make it on the live circuit and not just commit to PA's. You don't get the same emotion with a PA and if you're inexperienced it ruins a performance and the lyric.

SURNAME
Mr/Mrs/Miss ....

Age if under
12 years
INITIALS AND ONE FULL FORENAME

yrs. : mths.
Address...

Pharmacy Stamp

Pharmacist's pack & quantity endorsement	No. of days treatment N.B. Ensure dose is stated	NP	Pricing Office use only

Signature of Doctor | Date

For pharmacist No. of Prescns. on form

Warwickshire F.P.C.
DR. B. S. SIDHU,   880298
The Surgery Chancery Lane,
Chapel End,
NUNEATON.
Tel: 394788

IMPORTANT: Read notes overleaf before going to the pharmacy.   Form FP10 (Rev. 88)

Dr Sidhu's original lyrics to *I've Fallen For A Queen*. Right: Kalayan, percussionist for the Old Skool band Alaap.

2 The British Bhangra live music scene

Boy Chana and Rajinder Dudrah

My (Boy Chana's) first-ever experience with live British Bhangra was when I was about ten-years-old. We were invited to a family party at Aston Manor School in Newtown, Birmingham. I had been to many parties and celebrations but on this occasion I was inspired to take up drumming afterwards – even if it was on the table tops and doors of my then primary school, Lozells Junior and Infants – much to the dismay of the school caretaker! What had prompted me to bang away was seeing a young boy (Gurcharan Singh Fagura), barely older than myself, playing the bongo drums like nothing else mattered to him. He was a member of the **Bhujhangy Group** and that was an amazing sight. The scene ignited a passion in me for live British Bhangra music.

Live Bhangra music in Britain can be traced back to when young South Asian men held impromptu 'sing-a-long' events in the local pubs, particularly on the weekends when they returned from their hard manual work in the industrial factories of 60's and 70's Britain. This aspect of the early live scene is something that I would have loved to have experienced but sadly my parents seldom socialised due to my father's blindness, and I was too young at the time to be seen in a pub. From the pubs, and in the 80s, a live music scene began to emerge which brought together singers, musicians and audiences in club venues up and down

the country. Behind the development of this live scene were the current leaders of British Asian businesses who were then the first generation of Asian student audiences of live Bhangra. Some were born in India and had migrated with their parents to better their lives and gain a British higher education. Others were British born and bred.

It was at the British higher educational establishments, most notably the former polytechnics, where young students met each other and informally instituted the transformation from Punjabi folk music to British Bhangra. Bands like **Alaap**, **Chirag Pehchan**, **DCS**, **Heera**, **Premi** and others were all part of this emerging musical club culture. Key in bringing together the bands and audiences at venues were

A selection of Bhangra concert posters from the 80s and 90s. Below: Heera promotional poster, St George's Hall, Bradford, 1987.

promoters of the live music events, and student organisers from Asian societies at universities.

One such maverick promoter was **Gurd Chahal** who was educated in the 70s. He witnessed the live pub 'sing-a-long' scene through his father, and also worked with the likes of Alaap and Chirag Pehchan during their prime years in the mid-to-late 80s. Gurd is now semi-retired from his chosen career as a pharmacist, after building up successful pharmacies across the Midlands and Staffordshire. He is affectionately known as the man behind **Chahalco Promotions**, one of the first entertainment promotion companies that were aimed at young British Asian students in the 80s

and 90s, through live gigs at club events throughout the UK. Before Gurd established himself as a professional promoter of Bhangra concerts he also played a part in providing a regular framework for the performance of live music, which Bhangra bands of the 70s were able to partake in. As he explains, starting from his Disco roots in Walsall during the 70s:

A lot of the big promoters in the mainstream came from Walsall – MCP Promotions are one of the best in the country and Lobster Promotions were huge. When I went to Walsall College I had loads of friends who were into the Disco tunes of our time and me and my brothers formed companies to promote these events. We use to make money

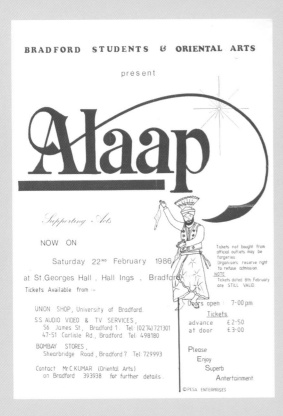

Bhangra concert posters from the 80s and 90s. Below: Member of Alaap playing live on stage, 1987.

out of these gigs and then me and my brothers decided to put on Asian cultural events, but we would lose money on these as the people were not used to large family type events. We would book a Town Hall and the bands would not be paid because there was a respect between promoters and bands and not a hierarchy; they needed us to make sure people knew about them and their talents. It was for the love of hearing your own music and bringing people together to appreciate the music. The first few bands we had played Hindi film music and the forming of Bhangra bands came along in the late 70s, like Bhujhangy and Anari Sangeet Party who used to cater for the local small pub venue. We took them away from that scene for a moment, but they always had the wedding market which they would never stop.

Even now you try and get Malkit Singh to stop doing the wedding circuit, it will be a straight 'no!'. But then the Asian teenagers came of age and we capitalized on the contact we had with the mainstream Disco scene.

29

HAMMERSM

PALAIS

HAMMERSMITH

Gurd's professional approach to organising live Bhangra music events drew on his experience of working with the white- and Asian-British music scenes respectively and bringing together the best of both worlds. This included introducing a smart dress code, an informed door policy, security at all events, hi-tech lighting, and extra entertainers in addition to the music artists, to create a memorable night out. The Chahalco banner started to grow in the mid-to-late 80s and Gurd showcased live Bhangra music with pomp and pageantry in key clubs of the period like the **Hammersmith Palais** in London, **Rotters Nightclub** in Manchester, and **The Dome** in Birmingham. He worked regularly with local promoters to arrange and ensure the success of live events. Perhaps the mainstay venue for Chahalco gigs was The Dome nightclub in Birmingham. The 30- and 40-somethings of today who attended at least one live show might well remember this venue as a milestone in their younger Bhangra clubbing life.

Gurd was also part of the daytime Bhangra scene. This developed out of the success of late evening and weekend events, the popularity of which spread by word of mouth and through Asian radio stations and press to youth across the country. In certain cases however, young people were unable to attend these late evening shows. The new 'daytimers' or 'daytime Bhangra discos'

Behind the development of this live scene were the current leaders of British Asian businesses who were then the first generation of Asian student audiences of live Bhangra.

as they came to be known, were therefore welcomed by sections of British Asian youth, but not always by other conservative sections of British Asian society (see also Chapter 4). Daytime events allowed British Asian youth to partake in British popular culture in terms of their own needs and desires. As Gurd explains:

> The daytime scene was something which kinda just happened. We saw what was happening with the small scale events in pub rooms and small clubs. We decided to do a row of daytime gigs at the biggest clubs in the UK. At the start there was a lot of sensitivity about holding parties in the daytime. There were already groups of

Punjabi boys making sure that any small scale events were stopped and it was a challenge for us to work with the community on something that they really didn't know about until we got involved. 'Will the students play truant?' was the main question on the minds of parents, and the other question of course was the female and male interaction under the influence of alcohol. We didn't want to encourage that, but here was a social phenomenon – Bhangra was socially and musically a phenomenon. It was important that we did not get into the bad records of the parents for the wrong reasons so we did tread very carefully. The radio stations of the time also picked up on the events and it was not just the Asian shows, the mainstream radio shows picked up on these 'daytimers'. On the positive side, the events were held on a Wednesday afternoon when it was half-day at college. Although the parents thought that their kids were at college every day of the week. Even though it started quite nicely we were getting the students who weren't on half-days and the police and authorities would have stopped the evening gigs. We were a victim of our own success! We ran it for a few months then we decided that the balance was just too tight to continue it.

Under Chahalco Promotions, Gurd has even acted as an adviser to some of the younger artists and bands of the late 80s and early 90s, assisting them to profile their music, appearance, personality and attitude so as to be in dialogue with their audiences. He remembers with affection, looking back through his personal photo memorabilia and personal recollections, one teenager in particular during the 80s, **Talvin Singh** (now of the album *Anokha* fame) who was often seen with Alaap backstage at the Hammersmith Palais at Chahalco's shows. Gurd cherishes having been around 'the best' bands on the live music scene during the heydays of live British Bhangra music and having had lots of good spirited fun. He even set up his own awards show to honour the early pioneers of the Bhangra scene:

The Bhangra Accolades were organised when the Pop Awards were waning…so what I worked on and organised was the Accolades…we brought in Jamla Jat (bless his soul, he is not with us anymore) to present the awards and he was given the top award. I brought him and also flew in Gurdas Maan and I remember Gurdas Maan fell to Jamla Jat's feet and said to me, 'Why have you flown me all the way from India when you have Jamla Jat here?'. It was a fantastic evening. We even brought in Page 3 girls to hand out the awards alongside Jamla Jat.

Another personality important to mention here is **Amarjit Sidhu** from the Midlands. Amarjit has been involved in the live and recorded British Bhangra music scene since the late 70s. He has been a band member of one of the first popular Birmingham Bhangra bands, Chirag Pehchan (Recognise the Light). During the 80s he was Manager of various popular British Bhangra bands such as **Apna Sangeet** (Our Music) from Birmingham, as well as producing a number of solo albums. During the 1989 Asian Pop Awards held at the Tower Ballroom in Birmingham, Amarjit was presented with the 'Best Personality Award' in British Bhangra music, in recognition of his continuous work to promote the British Bhangra industry. People like Gurd Chahal and Amarjit Sidhu have been important in giving time and entrepreneurial energy to the live music scene during the heydays of British Bhangra.

The Dome logotype. Overleaf: Alaap live in London, 1987.

3 Album sleeves

Rajinder Dudrah

The covers of British Bhangra albums are visually stunning and eye-catching, produced at particular moments in the development of British Bhangra's musical history. A closer look at the some of the sleeve art allows us to illustrate British Bhangra's story not only through the lyrics and the music, but also through its accompanying visuals and motifs.

Mick St Clair, *Bhangra Top 10: Non-Stop Remixes* (cover detail), Oriental Star, 1993.

Wicked & Wild
...eet Kondal
...USIC
...HAZANCHI
HOLLE
HOLLE

BALLY SAGOO
STAR-Y CRAZY

BHANGRA
MUFFIN'
SAT RANG

Saint Records

PREMI
Mein Tere Hogayee
MUT-1019
RECORDED IN 24 TRACK STUDIO

Alaap

BEAT THE RHYTHM
BALLE - BALLE

HEERA

ਜਗਦੀਪ ਸਿੰਘ
ਜਗਦੀਪ ਸਿੰਘ
ਜਗਦੀਪ ਸਿੰਘ
ਜਗਦੀਪ ਸਿੰਘ

...eep Singh Who's Gonna Love You?

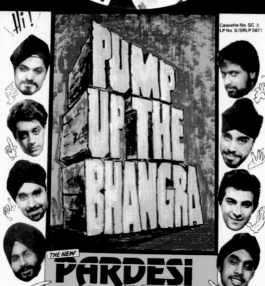

Cassette No. SC 5.
LP No. S/SRLP 5077
PUMP UP THE BHANGRA
THE NEW
PARDESI
MUSIC MACHINE

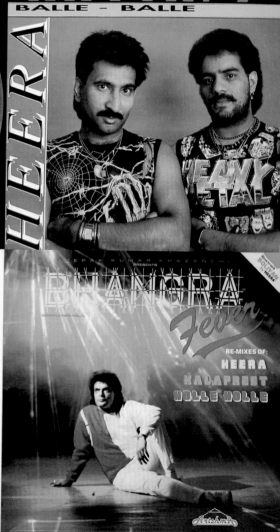

...EEPAK KUMAR KHAZANCHI
PRESENTS
BHANGRA Fever
RE-MIXES OF:
HEERA
KALAPREET
HOLLE HOLLE

SHAVA SHAVA
Kala Preet
ਸ਼ਾਵਾ ਸ਼ਾਵਾ
MUSIC BY DEEPAK KHAZANCHI

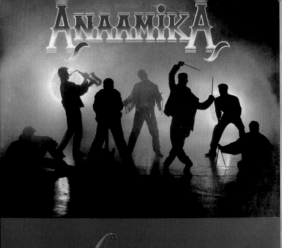

ANAAMIKA
Anonymous
THE DEBUT BHANGRA ALBUM
DIGITAL STEREO

MEET THE SAINT
NICK ST. CLAIR
THE CRUCIAL ALBUM

azaad joban
ਆਜ਼ਾਦ ਜੋਬਨ

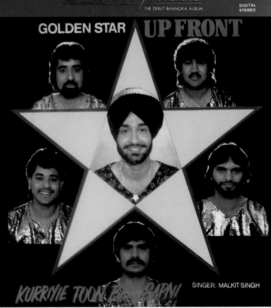

GOLDEN STAR UP FRONT
KURRIYIE TOON ... GARNI
SINGER: MALKIT SINGH

ਗਿੱਧੇ ਵਿਚ ਨੱਚ ਕੇ ਵਿਖਾ ਦੇ ਬੱਲੀਏ,
ਭੁੱਤੰਗੀਆਂ ਦੀ ਹੋਸ਼ ਭੁਲਾ ਦੇ ਬੱਲੀਏ
bhuyhangy group (u.k)
ਭੁੱਤੰਗੀ ਗਰੁਪ (ਯੂ ਕੇ)

BHANGRA TIME VOL 2
S/SRLP 5082
RANI SOHO ROAD DEE
Singers: BALBIR & DALBIR
Backing Vocals = Jassal Sisters

MASTI
GURDAS MAAN
ਮਸਤੀ ਗੁਰਦਾਸ ਮਾਨ
EMI STEREO

MAHENDRA KAPOOR
ਮਹਿੰਦਰਾ ਕਪੂਰ
BHABI GAL NA KARI
ਭਾਬੀ ਗੱਲ ਨਾ ਕਰ

Alaap • 'Dance With Alaap' • (1982 • Multitone)
Here, members of the London-based Alaap group stand proudly together fronted by their main singer Channi Singh. Alaap are one of the early pioneers of the British-based Bhangra sound: incorporating traditional Indian percussion instruments and lyrics with Western synthesized sounds and modern rhythms. Their track *Bhabiye ni Bhabiye* (Sister-in-law, oh sister-in-law), an ode by a younger brother-in-law who playfully pleads with his brother's wife to find him a marriage partner, has become an oft-requested classic at wedding parties.

By the early to mid-80s, British Bhangra albums were being sold in their thousands through specialist Asian music and video shops that were predominantly located in multicultural high streets of British cities. Album sleeves of the 80s were about marking presence and announcing one's arrival on the British Bhangra scene. The images of

these early album covers can be characterised in two ways. First, they can be seen as following in a line of post-war Black British portrait photography that marked the arrival of Black and South Asian settlers to Britain as securing paid jobs and accumulating material goods.[1] Secondly, that the album covers are telling of the moment – they are witness to the emergence of a section of British South Asian youth culture that engages with modern times.

In this sleeve, the five men are smartly dressed in suits or waistcoats and trousers. They are wearing a dress code that marks them as Western and modern. The lead singer, Channi, strategically shows off his gold chain and medallion and his silver watch. The uniformity of the men's attire also gives them their group identity – as the band Alaap. The sleeve also shows the workings of the British Bhangra music industry. Often band members would prove mobile, moving between different bands to assist with different musical productions, or to form new bands of their own. In the top left of the image we see Manjit Singh Kondal who after his time with Alaap went on to lead the group Holle Holle as their main singer.

1 The photographs by the Handsworth-based artist Vanley Burke are a good example of this kind of Black British portrait photography, a collection of which is housed in Birmingham Central Library.

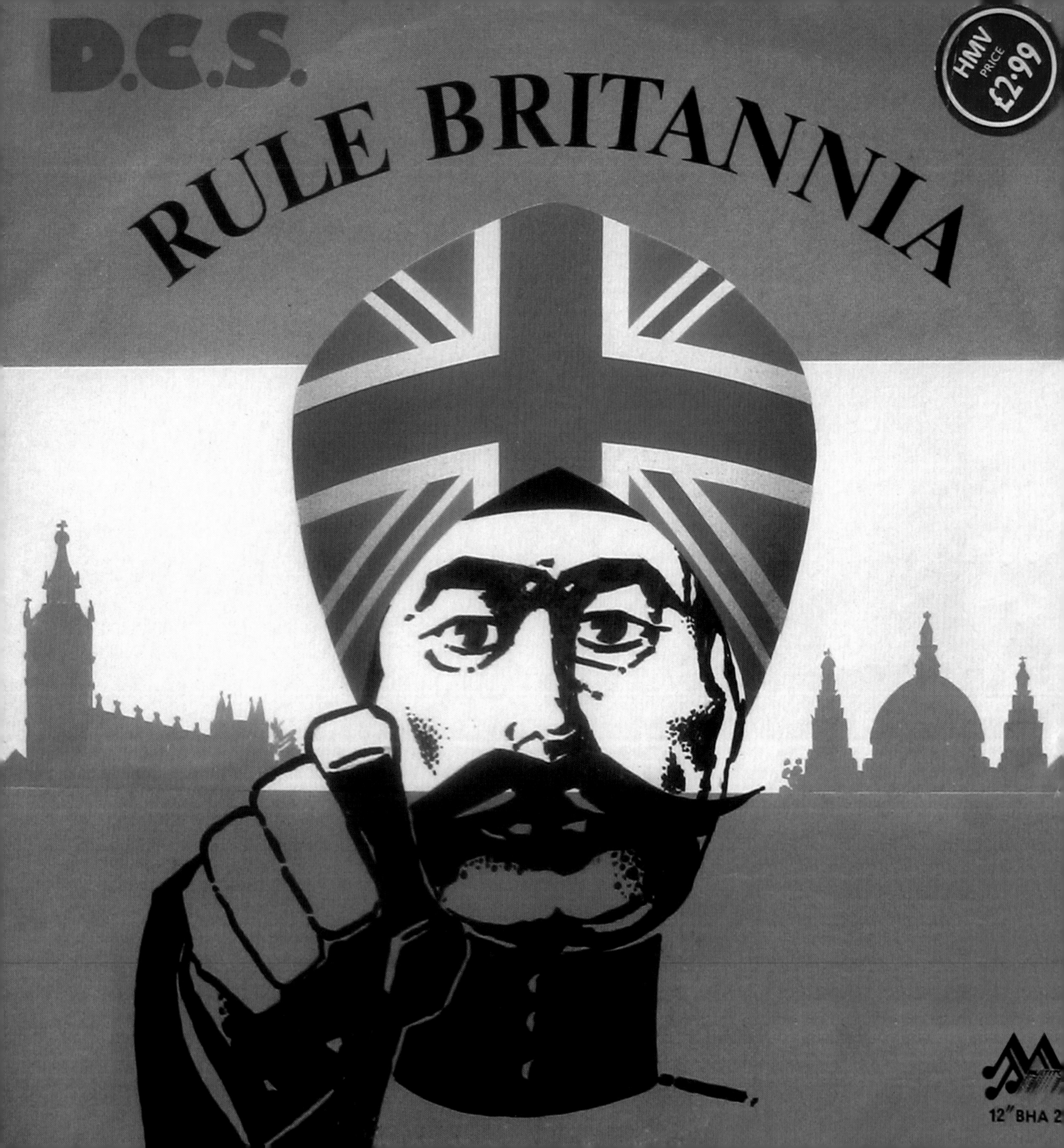
D.C.S.
RULE BRITANNIA
HMV PRICE £2·99
12" BHA 2

DCS • 'Rule Britannia' • (1991 • Multitone)

With 'Bhangra fever' gripping South Asian youth across the country by the late 1980s, some bands attempted to crossover into the mainstream charts, including Birmingham's DCS with their 1991 track *Rule Britannia*. The song was a call for national racial unity: 'We all live under the same sky, the same moon, so let's dance to the same old tune'. Such endeavours were unsuccessful, primarily because of the cultural racism encountered by British Bhangra artists when faced by the mainstream music industry. Their albums sold in thousands, mainly through South Asian music retail outlets. Yet the sale returns from these smaller stores were not included, or even acknowledged, in the make up of the British pop charts of the time. This is still the case.

'We all live under the same sky, the same moon, so let's dance to the same old tune'

In spite of the set backs faced by British Bhangra artists during the 80s, they continued to thrive as a sub-culture in relation to the mainstream pop charts. The music and lyrics of this period provided a source of popular culture and alternative politics from which sections of British Asian youth drew their inspiration and to which they contributed. Yet, the 70s and 80s was rife with debates in the mass media and at social policy levels about British Asian youth as 'caught between two cultures'. Implied within this discussion was that these youths were unable to decide whether they were British or Asian. However, Bhangra music combined mixed heritages and a variety of black, Asian, and Western genres, and indicated that Brit-Asian youths were able to manage a number of different cultural references and identities at the same time.

In this context, the album sleeve for *Rule Britannia* captures a sense of the music, its producers and audiences as collaborating in the call for belonging to notions of Britishness with aspects of their South Asian cultural heritages intact. The image is a reworking of the three colours from the Indian national flag. Imposed upon these colours is an adaptation of a poster that was very popular during the World War effort years – 'Your Country Needs You' (originally designed by Alfred Leete) – which called upon British men and women to actively partake in the war effort. Yet, the image of the central figure has been revised by identifying him as a British subject with South Asian roots – he wears a turban that is emblazoned by the Union Jack. On either side of him are the outlines of buildings: on the left, Big Ben and the Houses of Parliament and on the right, St Paul's Cathedral and Nelson's Column in London. Taken together, the sleeve draws upon a series of connected histories and identities and offers them in the context of late 80s British South Asian youth culture. This culture, then, is not only a production of the related histories of British colonialism in South Asia, the migration and settling of South Asians to Britain in the post-war period, but it is also a culture that will thrive and flourish if both British and Asian aspects work together.

Teri Yaad Aaye Ae
ਤੇਰੀ ਯਾਦ ਆਈ ਐ

Surinder Kaur
Live in Canada
Also Featuring
Jagjit Singh Zirvi

Music: Prem Gupta

STEREO

**Surinder Kaur • 'Teri Yaad Aaye Ae'
(Memories of You) • (1978)**

Women artists have been present since the start of British Bhangra music from its folk derivations in the Punjab to its present status as an urban anthem in Britain. For example, the female singers and sisters Surinder Kaur (pictured above) and Parkash Kaur from India were immensely popular folk singers during the 60s and 70s, and even toured Britain on a number of occasions for stage shows. With their powerful voice tones and folk sonnets they often questioned the predicament of women in heterosexual love relationships in which men were primarily considered as the source of a woman's heartache. Other female folk artists of the post-war period included Jagmohan Kaur and Narinder Biba. Their songs often criticised family structures and politics in which women had to negotiate a number of roles from housewife, lover, daughter-in-law, to matchmaker, and at the same time to create a space for themselves of their own. Their songs remain inspirational even for today's artists and bands and provide material for numerous cover versions. Admittedly, the histories and development of women's involvement in British Bhangra music remains to be charted comprehensively (see Chapter 5).

In this album cover, for recordings of Surinder Kaur's live performances in Canada, Kaur is dressed in a traditional white Punjabi dress, the salwar kameez, which is embroidered with red and black floral designs. She stands, almost angel-like, half-smiling, looking out through a window and up towards the skies. This image presents Kaur as an artist who is associated with her melodic voice and folk lyrics as offering a space for the female point of view to air her highs and lows on life. Kaur is also stood on the inside of the frame of the window; she is in the domestic setting looking out. As suggested by the title of the album, she is perhaps contemplating memories of a loved one or even contemplating new horizons. In this way, Kaur's album cover combines with the audience's knowledge of the lyrical content of her work as an artist that offers Bhangra listeners outside of the Punjab an imagined connection with the motherland and, at the same time, new beginnings in the place of settlement abroad. In the 70s, it was commonplace for British Asian men to be out working while women would predominantly work from home or attend to daily household chores. Thus, in this context, the female artist is celebrated and also photographed as an emblem of cultural mediation between the homeland and her adjusting to a new environment in the diaspora.

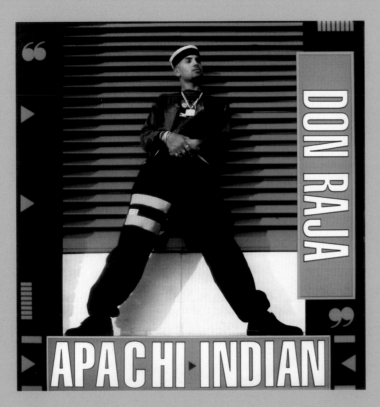

Apache Indian • 'Don Raja' • (1992 • Jet Star)

Apache Indian (also known as Steven Kapur) was the first British South Asian artist to break into the British music charts, Reggae Dance charts, and the South Asian music charts simultaneously in 1993 with his single *Arranged Marriage*. This track enabled him to launch a successful career as an international singer.

Apache Indian cannot simply be classified as a British Bhangra artist as his musical influences not only draw heavily on the Bhangra beat but also on Caribbean derived Ragga music. In several of his radio and television interviews during the mid-90s he has stated that musically and commercially he does not want to be identified solely as a Bhangramuffin (the term given to the combination of Bhangra and Ragga music). The music of Apache Indian illustrates the complex and hybrid interplay of music styles, lyrics and cultural identities that constitute the experience of young South Asians in urban locales. Apache's music in particular has its roots in the multicultural inner city area of Handsworth in Birmingham where he was raised; and like the diverse multi-ethnic make up of the place, his music is a combination of languages, rhythms and beats from across the Caribbean, North America, India and Europe. Apache's lyrics are rapped in the styles of Jamaican patois, Punjabi *boliyaan* (couplets), as well as in a culturally diverse urban street English.

In this album sleeve for *Don Raja*, Apache is placed centrally within the image as a young artist and multicultural ambassador. Born of Hindu Punjabi parents and visibly identifiable as a young Asian man through his brown skin colour, Apache 'mixes' his South Asian identity and cultural heritage through his attire, which draws on his musical upbringing and roots in Handsworth via Africa and the Caribbean. He wears a traditional African flat round cap, 'bling' gold and black lace chains which are adorned with different African and Indian unity symbols, and a slack, loose-fitting urban sweatshirt and stylish baggy trousers. His legs are astride and protrude from the image in the foreground as they form an A-shape that signifies his stage name – Apache. He casually leans back against a red and white background that, together with the bold horizontal and vertical lettering and symbols that display his name and album title, mark the sleeve as modern and contemporary within an urban context.

Album sleeves not only advertise the album or single as a product for sale from the British Bhangra music and cultural industry; they also visually encode meanings about the music genre, its artists and their combined histories. The images are produced by photography, by hand, and computer software technology to adorn LPs (long play records), cassette tapes and more recently CD covers and their related publicity.

4 The representation of Bhangra in the British media

Rajinder Dudrah

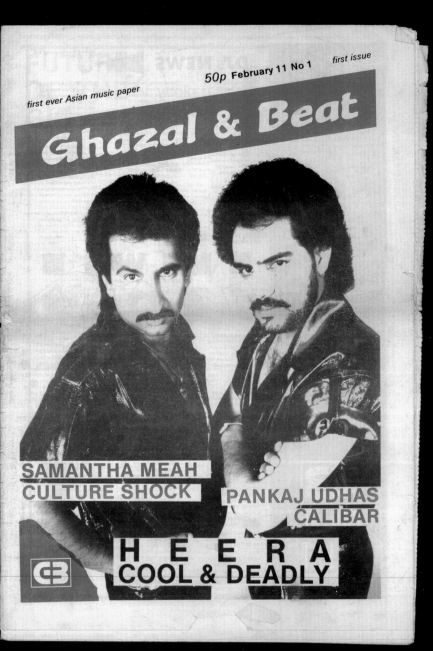

From the mid-1980s, British Bhangra began to be represented in media and academic accounts. What was known of early British Bhangra, that is Old Skool Bhangra, was little understood outside of its British South Asian audiences – at worst it was heavily caricatured in the media. Since the 90s, an emerging generation of British South Asian media practitioners, researchers and academics have been able to offer a more developed discussion of British Bhangra (see Sharma, Hutnyk, and Sharma 1996; and Dudrah 2002; 2002a)[1]. This chapter considers some of the early mainstream media reporting of British Bhangra and the ways in which it portrayed those young British South Asians who took part in Bhangra music activities.

Popular mainstream media accounts of British Bhangra: mid-to-late 8os

In 1986 the first mainstream popular media accounts of British Bhangra began to appear. These included a small feature in the popular youth magazine *The Face* in its March issue (see Banerji and Baumann 1990; and Huq 1996). In one sense, these accounts can be presented as 'discoveries' of British Bhangra music as part of an emerging South Asian youth culture. The media, however, were simply late in reporting a cultural experience that had existed for many years. British South Asian youth cultures did not only come into being in the mid-80s. As the popularity of Bhangra music and club scenes increased, so did the curiosity of white mainstream media towards British

South Asian youth culture; although their representation of South Asian youth was questionable. As Baumann noted of the early reporting of British Bhangra: 'Not all of this publicity was welcome for apart from its often patronizing tone, its pictures of a new generation of Asian youth regularly bunking off school to attend live shows created images that did justice neither to parents' attitudes nor to youngsters' aspirations' (Baumann 1990: 146). These tabloid attitudes are particularly characteristic of the media reporting of the mid-to-late 80s and early 90s.

The media tended to portray South Asian youth as repressed. *The Spectator* magazine, a serious publication which catered for a conservative upper and middle-class readership, claimed to 'investigate the spread of Bhangra fever among young Asians in London' (Roy Kerridge, 2 April 1988: 17–20). The article argued, incorrectly, that most of the London Bhangra youth lived in the East End of London. Why were West London's Bhangra revellers missing from this account?

The Asian Weekly review of the UK Bhangra Music Industry Awards, 1993. Left: *Ghazal and Beat* – Britain's first-ever Asian music paper, 1988.

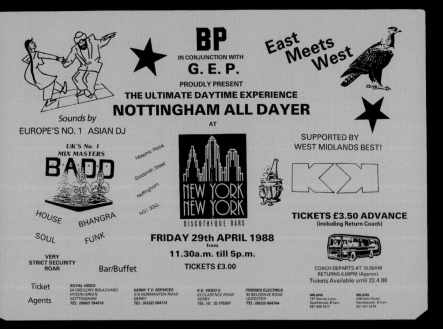

In the imagination of its readers, the use of the label 'East End' would have resonances, as the 'East', as a counterpoint to the 'West', could be portrayed as an alien land. The article describes a young Pakistani male as follows: 'He too seemed half of the East, half of the East End'. The restraints imposed by a restrictive culture and strict parents allegedly created a state of mental crisis for young people. Through its use of generalisations and stereotypes the article suggests that Bhangra dances provided a form of escape for South Asian youth from their 'internal problems'. The article goes on to say:

> It is odd to think that some of them have been formally betrothed in marriage to partners in India from the age of six. What is the preoccupation of these East End youngsters? Clearly they lead very intense lives, balanced on an invisible see-saw between parental approval and Things That Must Be Kept Secret From Home [writer's own emphasis]. Compulsory education has released the girls from the protective house-captivity their parents might wish to impose. But school plays only a small part in their lives, except as a social centre. Teachers are incapable of understanding their many problems. Unknown to grown-ups of any nationality, many of the youngsters slip away to the intoxicating, brightly-lit, romantic world of Bhangra dances.

Daytime Bhangra flyers.
Right: Article from *Asian People*, 1992.

The 90s and 00s: Bhangra moves on

By the mid-90s and thereafter, representations such as these were being challenged through the work of Bhangra artists, the arrival of cable and satellite TV channels, the growth of Brit-Asian radio stations and the British South Asian press that regularly reported Bhangra album releases and gigs. Mainstream white media industries rarely covered these alternative stories of Bhangra's importance for sections of British Asian youth.

The media tended to focus on the repressed-South Asian-youth angle. In a favourite conservative and middle-class read, 'The Spectator' magazine issued an article that claimed to "investigate the spread of Bhangra fever among young Asians in London".

+ASIAN SHOWBUSINESS EXTRA+

Poll plan to boost sales of Apachi's new record

PEOPLE REPORTER

REGGAE star Apachi Indian has hit on a revolutionary new idea to get maximum exposure in Asian households around the world.

An exclusive worldwide census has been commissioned to find out exactly where Asians live, to help target record sales.

It is the first time such a project has been carried out in the music industry.

A management spokesman said: "We have spent loads of money and time trying to make sure this information is spot on.

"Apachi could be the biggest in the world, but his records might not be getting to enough people.

"This information will help us to target Asian areas.

"But, if people really want to help him hit the big time, then they are going to have to make sure that they buy records in the shops that provide the figures for the charts."

His plea to Apachi's fans was "Please buy records from the top stores."

Apachi, who used to be a Birmingham welder, will be releasing a new single in the autumn called Arranged Marriages.

The track was played exclusively for The People last night – and we're predicting it is destined to be a smash hit.

The single will be followed by an album that will be released before the end of the year.

That will include a brilliant collaboration with top reggae star Maxi Priest.

Apachi said: "That album is going to be brilliant.

"All the people who have been asking 'Where is Apachi?' had just better watch out."

CENSUS SCHEME: Apachi Indian

TV Asia looks to The People

TOP executives of TV Asia revealed last night that one of the biggest reasons they decided to launch their satellite station was the Asian edition of The People.

The station directors said The People's venture was filling a major gap in the market.

A spokeswoman said: "What The People is doing is very important and a major step for the Asian community. I think TV Asia and The People can work hand-in-hand to give Asians in Britain and Europe exactly what they want, but cannot get from the mainstream organisations."

★ TOP ASIAN VIDEOS

HERE are this week's new top ten Asian video rentals:

1	(-)	**Kal Ki Awaz** Dharmendra, Raj Barbar
2	(-)	**Bol Radha Bol** Rishi Kapoor, Juhi Chawla
3	(1)	**Khel** Anil Kapoor, Madhuri
4	(2)	**Chamatkar** Shahrukh Khan, Urmila

No 1: Dharmendra

5	(3)	**Tahalka** Dharmendra, Naserudin Shah
6	(-)	**Mehboob Mere Mehboob** Boy Mukerjee, Pratibha
7	(7)	**Police Aur Mujrim** Raaj Kumar, Vinod Khanna
8	(8)	**Sapne Saajan Ke** Jackie Shroff, Karisma Kapoor
9	(-)	**Deedar** Ashay Kumar, Karisma Kapoor
10	(10)	**Deewana** Rishi Kapoor, Divya Bharti

★ TOP BHANGRA

HERE are this week's top ten Bhangra hits on Sunrise Radio:

1	(-)	**Bomb the Tumbi** Safri
2	(5)	**Traditional Boliyan** Various
3	(7)	**Hit That Dhol** Geet
4	(3)	**Never Mind The Dholaks** Satrang
5	(8)	**Hareepa** Cultural F X
6	(4)	**Dhol Attack** Bittu
7	(7)	**Feel Like A King** Ajuba
8	(6)	**Dhol Blasters** Various
9	(9)	**Dhol Banger** Manni
10	(10)	**Kickin Klassix** Surinder Shinda

★ TOP SONGS

THE most requested Asian film songs on Sunrise Radio last week were:

1	(1)	**Pehli Nazar** Pyar Hua
2	(2)	**Pyar Ho Jayega** Chamatkar
3	(-)	**Kya Kahun Aaj Lata** Teri Payal Mere Geet
4	(3)	**Aisi Diwaangi** Diwana
5	(7)	**Tumhe Dil To De Chuke** Mashooq
6	(6)	**Churaya Mera Dil** Laat Saab
7	(5)	**Sochenge Tumhe Pyar Karen Ke Nahin** Diwana
8	(-)	**Mohabat Ka Devta** Teri Payal Mere Geet
9	(-)	**Dil Diwaneka Dola** Tehelka
10	(-)	**Pehla Nasha** Jo Jita Wohi Sikander

HOLY BO

Fat into to

RAG lives life coo dutifully supposed

But no there and she plays the Musli

For Sal spend the compelled Islamic bo

★★ YOUR GUIDE TO ASIAN RADIO ★★

GEM (MW: 1260Khz) Nottingham, Leicester and Derby. Sunday: 7pm Don Kotak. Sabras Weekday: Mon: 6pm Chris Tailor. 10.0 Tilly Agravat. Tues: 6pm Don Kotak. 10.0 Anil Kapoor. Weds: 6pm Jay Khera. 10.0 Pravin Lukka. Thurs: 6pm Deedar Bahra. 10.0 TSR. Fri: 6pm Chris Tailor. 10.0 Sheila Kaur. Saturday: 6pm Jay Khera. 10.0 Anil Kapoor.

SUNRISE (212 M

Asian music. 9.0 Maher Khan-Raag se: Ghazal Tak. 11.0 Night-time with JK. 2am–5am Night Music. Pareveen Mirza. Weekdays: 6am Religious Programme. 7.0 Tony Patti. 9.0 Job Search. 10.0 Paul Davis. 12.0 Ravi Sharma. 2pm Parveen Mirza. 4.0 Parveen/ Tochi Chaggar. 5.0 Avtar Lit: sundown Show. 7.0 Tochi Chaggar. 9.0 Asian Mixed Music. (Mon: 10.0 Tamil Magazine. Tue, Wed: Gujerati Magazine). 11.0–6am

tional Rock Breakfast Show. 6pm Asian, with Asif Gazhali. 7.30–9.0 Bengali. Weekdays: 5am Dawn Traders with Jeet Bahal. 7.0–10.0 International Rock Breakfast Show. 6pm Asian with Asif Gazhali. 7.30–9.0 Bhangra Programme. Saturday: 5am Dawn Traders with Jeet Bahal. 7.0–10.0 International Rock Breakfast Show. 7.30pm – 9.0 Bhangra Programme.

rit Vani. 6.00 Harmony Breakfast Show. 9.00 Talkback. 11.00 Brunchbox. 1.00 Reggae Got Soul. 3.00 Drive In Harmony. 6.00 Asianwide. 8.00 Openline. 9.00 Bengali Sangeet. 10.00 YOu Don't Have To Be Irish. 11.00 Supermix. 1.00–5am Night Cap. Tues-Fri (same as Monday except the following): Tues: 9pm Gurjarati Sangeet. No Night Cap. Weds: 8pm Jharokha. Thurs: 8pm

End of term Daytime
Bhangra flyer with
promoter's disclaimer.

"Compulsory education has released the girls from the protective
house-captivity their parents might wish to impose. But school plays
only a small part in their lives, except as a social centre. Teachers
are incapable of understanding their many problems. Unknown to
grown-ups of any nationality, many of the youngsters slip away to the
intoxicating, brightly-lit, romantic world of Bhangra dances."

ROAR IN CONJUNCTION WITH B.P. PROMOTIONS

Presents

An END OF TERM

BHANGRAMANIA

ALL DAYER! on **FRIDAY JUNE 26th 1992** at the

HUMMING BIRD Dale End

SHOCKING OUT TO TOP BHANGRA, RAVE & REGGAE D.J.'s

BAD COMPANY (London)
EXECUTIVE (London)
D.J. Ace (B'ham)
HIGH FREQUENCY (Oxford)
EAST & WEST
KUT-D (B'ham)
RAGGA SINGH (B'ham)
D.J. BOS (B'ham)

DANCE TILL YOU DROP!

ATTRACTIONS:
MEGA BASS SOUND SYSTEM
UNIQUE LIGHTS AND VISUAL SYSTEM
PROJECTION-POWER STROBES
BACK DROPS-FLAVOURED SMOKE
RECORDS, CASSETTES & T-SHIRTS STALLS
DANCE COMPETITIONS
LOTS OF FREE PRIZES TO GIVE AWAY

TICKETS £4.00 IN ADVANCE

AVAILABLE FROM:
MILAN-Soho Road & Stoney Lane
ROMA-Soho Road,
HUMMING BIRD Box Office
ROMA MUSIC BANK-Soho Road

NO TRUBLE MAKES ALLOWED, NO DRUGS,
NO DRESS RESTRICTIONS
STRICT SECURITY BY R.O.A.R STRICTLY OVER 18's

SPECIAL NOTE: WE THE ORGANIZERS WOULD LIKE TO
STATE THAT IN NO WAY DO WE WISH TO ENCOURAGE TRU-
ANCY AND THEREFORE WE HAVE ORGANIZED THIS PARTY
ON THE LAST DAY OF TERM TO CELEBRATE THE END OF
EXAMS.

DOORS OPEN 12.00AM TO 5.00PM

A number of landmark events raised the global profile of the British Bhangra music industry and helped to shift the media reportage that the music had previously received. Alongside the continued work of British Bhangra artists, post-Bhangra artists such as **Apache Indian** and **Panjabi MC**, partly through their collaborations with international music producers and singers **Maxi Priest** and **Jay Z** in 1992 and 2002 respectively, attained critical recognition as their music broke new ground in terms of fusion-based styles. Coverage changed as the music of such artists entered Top Ten music charts globally and British Asian media professionals called for sophisticated and varied stories of members of their communities. No longer was British Bhangra portrayed as escapist music for people who were 'caught between two cultures' in the 1980s; instead, by the early 21st century, writers portrayed it as an experience which captured the multi-faceted layers of British Asian lives. British Bhangra music influenced many contemporary sounds: Bhangra remixes, UK Pop, commercial R'n'B, urban Rap, Garage, and Grime. The mix of musical genres and the diverse lives of their audiences are now starting to feature in media representations.

1 Music reviews, gig listings, and interviews with British Bhangra artists and bands in the popular British South Asian press (e.g. the Friday weekly UK newspaper *Eastern Eye*) and media (e.g. local, regional and international radio stations) are interesting counter-reference points. The World Wide Web is also a medium where Bhangra enthusiasts from across the South Asian Diaspora, but most notably from Britain and North America, have been able to demonstrate the growing popularity of the music. During the heydays of British Bhangra, media outlets such as the BBC TV programme *Network East* and the former magazine *Ghazal and Beat* were alternative sources of information.

Pop Goes Punjabi newspaper article. Overleaf: Boy Chana's media archive.

4

The Bhangra Beatwave is taking Asian discos by storm, reports Sheryl Garratt. Photographs by John Arthur

POP GOES PUNJABI

Outside, it's three o'clock on a sunny spring-afternoon in London's Leicester Square. Shoppers and tourists bustle by, unaware of the mayhem just through the doors of London's Empire Ballroom. Inside, it's the heat that hits you first, then the noise. The walls drip with sweat from the 2,000 bodies moving to the latest soul and funk. Whistles and foghorns fill the air with shrill blasts of excitement, while the crowd sing along to the hook-lines of well known tunes. Boys strut and pose in groups, girls change into skimpy clothes and plaster on makeup in the loos. This could be any soul all-dayer, anywhere, except for one crucial difference - almost everyone here is Asian.

Sometimes banned from Western discos by protective parents, or turned away by racist bouncers, the young Asian community has set about organising clubs of their own. It's quite a culture shock at first to see someone getting down to James Brown in a sari. But that's nothing compared to the hysteria that breaks loose when the main attraction, a group called Heera, finally take the stage. Women strain forward in wild attempts to grab the singer's crotch. Men perform wobbly dances perched on each others shoulders. Undies are passed onstage, and a circle forms around acrobatic dancers performing backflips that would make a Bronx breakdancer weep with envy. Welcome to the wonderful world of Bhangra. Originally a folk dance to celebrate a successful harvest in the Punjab, Bhangra has been taken up by the new generation. Bhangra bands are springing up all over the place, and the top names regularly attract crowds of thousands in discos across the country. Until now, it has been a secret movement, growing invisibly in the clubs and halls - there's an Asian community. Records sell tens some groups even have gold discs to mainly through Indian shops. Events are publicised the only

Heera, (above) Insets: rave it boogie

"Bhan music of po "Peop parti unde

disco. Then they started denly Bhangra fever too "Five to ten years ago they were rubbish as m of competition now, pe music is moving forwa the kids. There us tended

THE ASIA... WARDS S...

...OY CHANA REPORTS LIVE FROM THE DOME AF...
...SIC INDUSTRY'S MOST-EAGERLY AWAITED EVENT

stage to present **Johnny Zee** with the award for the best album cover design for 'Vibes'. Young Johnny was so happy that he did a little jig there and then on stage!

The **Pardesi** lads couldn't have been more pleased with their award for the best song (Putt Jatan De). The delighted boys let out the Sikh victory cry which echoed around the Dome.

Up until this point the crowd were very responsive, but unfortunately they showed their disapproval when they didn't like an act. Poor **Najma Akhtar** received the award for Best Female Singer. And when she went on to sing two songs the

...gets his dues from Amrita Singh
...the trophy was a mighty thing.
...th waves and a kind of figure,
...like the Oscar, but we'll call it **The**
Amarjit. The awards which
Johnny Zee (Hit The Deck),
Heera (Cool and Deadly - they
didn't even bother turning up to
collect it, by the way), **Azaad**
...Golden Star (Hai Shava),
...Drum and Dholl, **Bali** (Patel Rap)
...when the real awards started
...nail-biting anticipation. The
...Female Newcomer' was
...ted by **Shin** from DCS to
...a, who was probably of
...male newcomer of

...the screams, for
...tress **Amrita Singh**
...age to present an

The 'Best International Male Singer' went to **Mangal Singh** who embraced **Malkit** as he collected the award.

The talent they had all been waiting for, **Gurdass Mann**, entered the stage on a lift - like a God - as the chorus line helped by **Apna Sangeet** belted out to the unmistakable tune of Challa. I could not believe I was in the presence of the great **Gurdass Mann** and that his voice was so powerful. The crowd surged forward in a great wave to catch a glimpse of him - a sight no other band had commanded that evening. You'll be glad to hear that he'll be back in December for a special live date at The Dome.

After singing 'Aakiyan Udee Dyan' he was whisked off in a shroud of security to the VIP

...he was followed by **G Mall** from **Nachda Sansaar**, who picked up the 'Best Bhangra Dance Group' award.

The 'Best Video' went to **Achanak's** 'Lak Nu Hala De' and 'Best Album' was awarded to **Alaap**, who were also absent, reportedly in Germany. Coming 'Best Up and Band' went to the favourites. The

Malkit proved a big hit with the crowd

restless audience almost shoved her off stage with their reaction. Canadian singer **Dal** also proved to be a turn-off for the crowd. Radio Derby's **Niki, Poli, Sati Kash**, better known as the **Asajkal Boys**, leaped on stage to grab the mike and show off their awful hair do's! In reverse order of their Best Male Singer' prize. To the delight of the crowd it went to **Malkit Singh**. However, young Malk was in another part of the Dome at the time which caused a bit of confusion as the sound his way to the stage **Sunrise Radio's Harkiratan Singh** kept them happy by announcing 'Muje Nend Na Aye' from the movie Dil, as 'Best International Song' and **dha Paudwal** as the 'Best international Singer'. At this kit arrived to a roar from

Surjit, still in bandages after an unexplained accident, came on stage to cries and cheers.

A new category for Innovative Band' went to **Anaamika**. But the award that everyone had been waiting for, 'The Best Live Band', deservedly, went to **Achanak**. The 'Best Band of 00/91' which an overjoyed **Pardesi** surged on stage ending the show with their 'Best Song' - 'Putt Jatan De'.

Amarjit Sidhu, a man who has worked hard and relentlessly for the show, deserves an award for the sheer effort he put into it. But afterwards he felt disappointed.

Surjit worked hard to make the event a success

The Sahotas entertain The Dome press lounge where he sat with Malkit signing autographs and the award. Back to the awards and the 'Best Lyricist' award went to KS Bhamra from Apna Sangeet.

BOY CHANA

...N FASTIC!

...CHANA talks to the boys
...at Frantic about the
...they call the 'Maniac'...

...ers due to the exactness
...of the vocals. Avtar's LP is
...full of extremes. Surinder
...Singh added a traditional
...touch to the album while
...the boys at Frantic gave it
...the funkier beats.

N Inder Johal, of Avtar's record company, Nachural, says: "Avtar Maniac's album is that I'm not sure how to deal with it. It will fare with our other albums and singles. I know how much to duplicate and send out. But Extreme has created a very difficult situation.

"The Maniac will be a shock to the system for both bhangra fans and artists. His voice stands out from every other artist

SURINDER: Met the Maniac by chance failed to give us a solution. For some reason they are keeping Avtar Maniac's real identity under wraps by refusing to issue his photographs.

So when they find a paper large enough to cover him, will they find a big head?

beats of Extreme I heard. Avtar was a kind and a half. I was due to meet a promoter to receive a record for a gig at Night Club, Birmingham. It was late and I wandered around and heard the sound of rehearsing with a player was my old friend Surinder Singh, who introduced me to him and the intro later, his album

A TO D...

...you don't know your dholak from your tumbi, read o...
...prehensive guide to bhangra but felt too stupid to a...
...now about the industry...

AREEPA! An intriguing word in most bhangra cen... it's all in the beat! We... Karpal, Chirag Pehchan, Cultural FX.

D is for **DHOL**, the big fat drum which gets everyone's ankles wav... ing in ecstasy. In recent years there have been unseen many albums which have had Dhol Blasters, Dhol Attack, Dhol Outburst, Living Dhol D's, Dhol Dulkus, Death Ja... Famous D's: DCS, Die hard... Deepak Khazanchi.

E is for **EASTERN EYE** the only publication which pri... and features bhangra in a... lary! What a East W... Famous E's: East W... Connection, Esharti, ... Boyz

F is for **FLAT...**

G... Famous G's: Cobra, Cowboy gaye... Karpal, Chirag Pehchan, Cultural Band, Gold... FX. Maan

H is t... over... dec...

MEAN MA...

BOY CHANA drinks to the long-awaited return of Birmingham's baddest band...

O RIGINALITY, madness and gallons of lager are the secret ingredients of Pardesi's spectacular success.

On their way to the top, they have... awards that have encouraged their footsteps.

up and states: "We have done a number of cover versions in the past and may do mo... But it is a fact that the major...

...CHANA DISCOVERS WHY SILINDER...'S NEW RELEASE WILL BE PLAYED ...URDWARAS AND NOT NIGHTCLUBS...

...the past few years, bhangra stars have taken a ...Achanak and Hans Raj Hans have taken Malkit ...rom dance music to highlight the role of ...casing religious LPs. ...bet quite unlikely artist, is turning his attention ...ha and the dhol and focussing on matters of a ...otherwise ...all one in ...ine, first ...ering for ..., which ...album, ...thank ...o had ...wanted to ...wara ...ven ...If ...a 16-track recording studio so I ...can use my free time to work on ...Hindi or ghazal albums. These

Pardesi, Silinder has teamed up with Frantc Productions to cre- ate another holy album, Mitter Pyare Noo.

"I've just set up a new compa- ny. Melody productions, and wanted to do something special to start me off," he continues. "The only way I will prosper is with the blessing of the Gods.

"Setting up Melody is some- thing that I had had in mind for a very long time, I've also acquired

Sitting in Silinder's home you can't help noticing how the walls, as in most Sikh homes, are adorned by illustrations of Sikh gurus. I asked Silinder what role religion played in his life.

"I am not a devoutly religious person," he replies. "This may be due to the line of work that I am in, but I try to pray whenever I can. I feel that without religion a person is hopeless as he or she has nothing to guide them.

"I'm not saying that we should all follow religion, but faith is the backbone of society. We must learn to understand what is written in the scriptures no matter which religion we belong to.

"For a man who se... more of... than o...

will commemorate the life of my heroes Mohammed Rafi and Mukesh," he adds. "In fact, Mitter Pyare Noo is a tribute to the late Mohammed Rafi as all the songs have previously been sung by him.

disappointed?

"People may say: 'Look at him. Before he was pumping up the bhangra and now he wants to pump up the prayer books!'" he laughs.

"But I have thought hard about this project, not just in selecting songs, but also in terms of the sentiments I should portray. It has taken me two years to research this album so I feel

> **'People may say: 'Look at him. Before he was pumping up the bhangra and now he wants to pump up the prayer books!'**

the album. The singer's foresight and religious beliefs have also meant that he has done the album off his own back. He paid the musicians himself, thanks to his friends Surinder and Kam of Frantic Productions, he has not been charged for the studio costs because they feel it's beneficial to them too.

"We hope that this album will bring us luck for years to come in our newly furbished studios," said Surinder.

Being young (well, younger than both Silinder and Kam), Silinder has included many things that young kids would want to know and understand.

"It's up to the kids of today to keep the religion of the forefathers going. The same could be said about Punjabi music in the form of bhangra. We keep it alive by playing to the kids. So why should- n't we record religious songs for the young- sters," asks Kam.

... record companies ...money at...

...HANGR... ...AS GOOD AS G...

we could have more songs o... this nature. Hint hint!!.

P is for PEENI, PEENI, PEENI. See S. Famous P's: Premi, Panja... MC, Pardesi Music Machi... Parmjit Pammi, Parwann... Sangeet, Paaras, Pataka... Powerhouse

Q is for QUEEN. Pri... Diana ne Sas Kutni.

...UD:A vital accessory ...try, which is about ...sidering makhan ...ns butter! ...Malkit Singh, ...Mala, Manni ...Singh.

No explana-
...b, Nachda
...jab
. If only
...waving your arm

R is for RAGGA, th... craze, which has bee... ing like wild fire since... arrival of the internal... acclaimed Mr Indian... known as Apache). Famous R's: Radio... Ragga Kaka Winst...

S is for SHARA... intoxicating subst... will rid you of all... you won't feel lik...

BOY CHANA finds out why Malkit Singh thinks he has the Midas Touch...

IT's been years since the last fantastic album emerged from the Kingstanding area of Birmingham. But the enigma surrounding the Mighty Malkit Singh still seems to render many people speechless.

There's no doubt that the shy guy is the hottest property on two legs since Linford Christie, as zillions of fans in places as far afield as Singapore, Thailand and Australia will tell you.

The super Singh's success is partly due to his choice of musicians. Their youthful vibes have influxed a great sense of energy into the tra- ditional shy man of bhangra. They have also influenced him to record and aim his ...est album, Midas Tou... his fans in England.

The LP, which g... release today, featur... which are normally ... ed with younger, m... bands, so this is ...

"Once my band had settled down, the senior members started pushing me to record an album here," he whispers. ...even't had the opportuni... ...hat since my debut ...the Vich and, ...ects with ...due

"Talks with Island were hap- pening at one point, but they wanted to release my album in December," he reveals. "I ... that this would be too ...my loyal fans to wait. ...eady comment- ...n absence ...t that

Playing alongside the likes of Safri and even young bands like Anakhi, Malkit saw that the crowd reaction to tradi- tional music was a big kick up the tumbi!

And this hasn't happened in England alone. Critics in India have also been gunning him down. But, because he is the most famous name on the circuit, mainstream record label, Island Records, have been knocking at his door.

...struggle to get booked up for a gig. Malkit is like a registry office on Valentine's Day! ...roduced his diary (for ...Singh was crammed ...ngs. Norway, These ...arm-

"There has never been any strict competition between Safri and myself as we have our own style. This rivalry was hyped up at a concert that Eastern Eye organised! Safri and I spoke about the matter and we both felt it was just a ploy to sell tickets. But the crowds thought other- wise."

Midas Touch is Malkit's 14th recording. While most bands today have one release and

> **'The rivalry between me and Safri was started by Eastern Eye's concert!'**

All of whom are his very good friends.

"One of the things that singers like Manak, Gurdass and I are against is the phase of cover ver- sions that have crept into the industry," says Malkit.

"I have never taken someone else's songs or tunes to parade in my record- ings. I hope I never will. This 'album tam- pering' is responsible for keeping our indus- try in the dhol-drums. As fans buy cassettes hoping for new mater- ial, they get songs done by someone else four weeks ear- ...er!"

The multi-talen... artiste, who has ... acted in a Pu... film, used six... for Midas To... has penned ... of songs h... "In usin... styles o... have cr... variet... that ... appr...

His first release near... made waves. Now,... MC is hoping his...

F ...ROM Cove...
...Singh...
...scen...

5 Women in Bhangra

Rajinder Dudrah

Mohinder K Bhamra.
Right: Sangeeta, *A breath of fresh Bhangra air*, Keda, 1990.

The story so far has been told predominantly through the narratives and experiences of men, but these were not the only voices in the music industry; women artists have been present since the birth of British Bhangra music. The Indian singers and sisters, **Surinder Kaur** and **Parkash Kaur**, as well as artists **Narinder Biba**, and **Mohinder Kaur Bhamra**, were immensely popular folk singers in the post-war period (see Chapter 3), and artists **Balbir Bobby**, **Parmjit Pammi**, **Kamaljeet Neeru** and **Sangeeta** released albums and sang live around the world during the 80s and early 90s.

These artists also performed and contributed to the genre of *Ghidda*, the female counterpart music to Bhangra.[1]

When the *Eastern Eye* newspaper ran a feature in 1996 asking 'Why is the Bhangra industry dominated by men?' ('Let's Talk About Sexism', *Eastern Eye*, 10 May 1996), Bina Mistry, a female artist based in London, replied:

> I think the world is very male-dominated – not just the Asian music industry or even the non-Asian industry at that. But it's all changing rapidly. Good music will always surface whether it's male or female led. This bias has always been there but I myself have never faced it directly, well not enough to make me want to cry – but I'm always whingeing about it.

The British Bhangra industry like any other sphere of media production led by men is open to charges of gender bias and sexism.[2] Yet an industry shaped and dominated by men, has also been transformed by the input of its women artists.

Women work in the Bhangra industry primarily as singers or professional dancers and only a few manage and promote music and artists. Bhushra Ahmed, for example, was the Head of Fruitcake Music in London, a record company that managed the female artist **Sabina** in the late 90s. There is no record as yet, of any

Sangeeta
A breath of fresh Bhangra air
Music Kuljit Bhamra

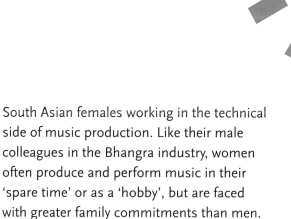

South Asian females working in the technical side of music production. Like their male colleagues in the Bhangra industry, women often produce and perform music in their 'spare time' or as a 'hobby', but are faced with greater family commitments than men.

Sameera and **Anupreeta**, two female artists, both described their entry into the Bhangra industry as a result of audience demand.[3] Both were keen to pursue their music interests by singing ballads and slow melodies ranging from popular Bollywood tracks to *Ghazals*. However, demand for British Bhangra led them to take up singing at live performances, and the recording of albums. Consequently female artists were entering a field of music in which men had a strong foothold:

Anupreeta: I enjoy singing more the 60's and 70's Lata Mangeshkar's [popular Bollywood playback singer] melodies. I had to learn Bhangra songs in order to respect the wishes of the audience.

Women had to perform British Bhangra if they were to be given exposure, and wished to move into singing other genres. This was particularly the case in the heyday of British Bhangra up to the mid-90s:

Sameera: I was introduced to Bhangra purely because the demand was for Bhangra in this country. It was thought I would sell better if I was able to sing in Punjabi and Bhangra tracks. If I was in Bombay, on the other hand, there would be more opportunities for me to sing perhaps in the film industry.

"The world is very male-dominated – not just the Asian music industry or even the non-Asian industry at that. But it's all changing rapidly. Good music will always surface whether it's male or female led."

Performing in a male-dominated industry led to notable differences in experiences between men and women.

Top sales figures of Bhangra albums are usually always held by men, after all there are more male artists in the industry than women, with more opportunities to produce and release albums and singles.[4] Sales are also related to audience expectations and listening habits. For instance, Ninder Johal signed Sameera to Nachural Records for the release of her first album *Infinity* in 1995. It did not perform as well as male-led albums on the market at the same time. The reason for its limited success is revealing:

Ninder: If there's a female artist on a Bhangra tape nobody wants to know. Why? Because it's seen as such a macho thing, women should not be singing those type of songs. Therefore the Asian market is holding female artists back. I invested in Sameera's album *Infinity*, it was a superb product, she sang really well. At the end of the day nobody wanted to know, they wanted something with a bit of Karakhaa!, which means a bit of aggression, a bit of noise, a bit of a bang, which only men can allegedly do.

Infinity was released at a time when most Bhangra albums featured loud and energetic tracks. *Infinity* was a break from the norm with tracks sung in Hindi as well as Punjabi, ranging from sweet melodies to *Ghazals* and Bhangra. Ahead of its time in terms of audience expectation, it also challenged notions of what was acceptable as an album of British Bhangra music.

It is not only in sales figures that there exists an imbalance of income generated by male and female artists. Money earned from album signing fees for the Bhangra industry are, on the whole, much less than for mainstream music genres – but women, despite being able to sing across a range of different music genres and vocal styles, are not able to command as high a price as their male counterparts. As the artists put it:

Sameera: The demand for Bhangra is more and men predominate. If I was a man I'd make more money.

Anupreeta: In terms of making money women have to struggle maybe three times more to survive in the industry. Not twice, but three times more I would say.

Sisters doing it for themselves: diversification of the Bhangra industry

These two experiences of the plight of women artists in the British Bhangra industry might reveal them as perpetual victims with little autonomy to bring about change. However, transformations have occurred within the industry since the heydays of Bhangra music with the emergence of young, fresh, and outspoken female talent, able to create their own niches.

By the mid-90s the Bhangra industry diversified, taking into account the popularity of Bollywood film music amongst its audiences. Bhangra albums began to

Dulku's, *Kuriyan Ku Kuriyan* (cover detail), Multitone Records.

Above: Sheni, contemporary Asian arts and music promoter in the North West of England. Below: The representation of women on Bhangra and Asian Pop sleeve art.

feature musical influences from Bollywood film tracks encompassing a range of South Asian music genres and the performance of Bollywood songs with a Bhangra feel to them at live gigs. The shift towards Bollywood remixes, *Ghazals* and *Qawallis* alongside Bhangra music, witnessed women coming into their own and taking charge of the reigns of music production in a number of respects. Female artists found that they had more autonomy to be able to sing on their own terms over a wider range of music genres:

Sameera: I have always been singing Hindi melodies and I think my voice is more suited to ballads. I consider ballads more difficult to sing than faster dance tracks because the slower you sing the more difficult it is to maintain the voice and keep it in tune over a stretch. Now that the Hindi remixes have come on the scene, I have gone back to what I really loved doing singing in Hindi, and that's where I feel I'm at my best.

Band management and young talent: sisters calling the shots

Bollywood remixes became a considerable market segment of the British Bhangra industry by the mid-90s and the contribution of women artists was taken seriously. The female singer of the live Hindi bands was often the one who headed the group and she also hired male musicians for performances at her own discretion. As the female artists **Shama**, and **Bharti**, who specialise in singing Hindi film tracks put it in response to the *Eastern Eye* newspaper's call 'Why is the Bhangra industry dominated by men?':

Shama: When I was a freelance singer it was a bit more difficult but now that I've got my own band – I call the shots! I employ the male artists and musicians; I've turned the tables.

Bharti: It's like another world in the Hindi market where it's almost vice-versa, I find that males struggle more than women! If you look at bookings for shows, in general, you'll find more females being approached by the organisers. Even though the musicians are male, the scene is controlled by women because 90 per cent of the time they've got their own set-ups and they employ or book the male singers.

The Bhangra industry diversified to include a wider repertoire of South Asian music genres. Women artists have moved into band management and new and younger talented performers in their late teens and 20s have emerged. Since the mid-to-late 90s, artists such as **Sasha**, **Sabina**, **Shabnam**,

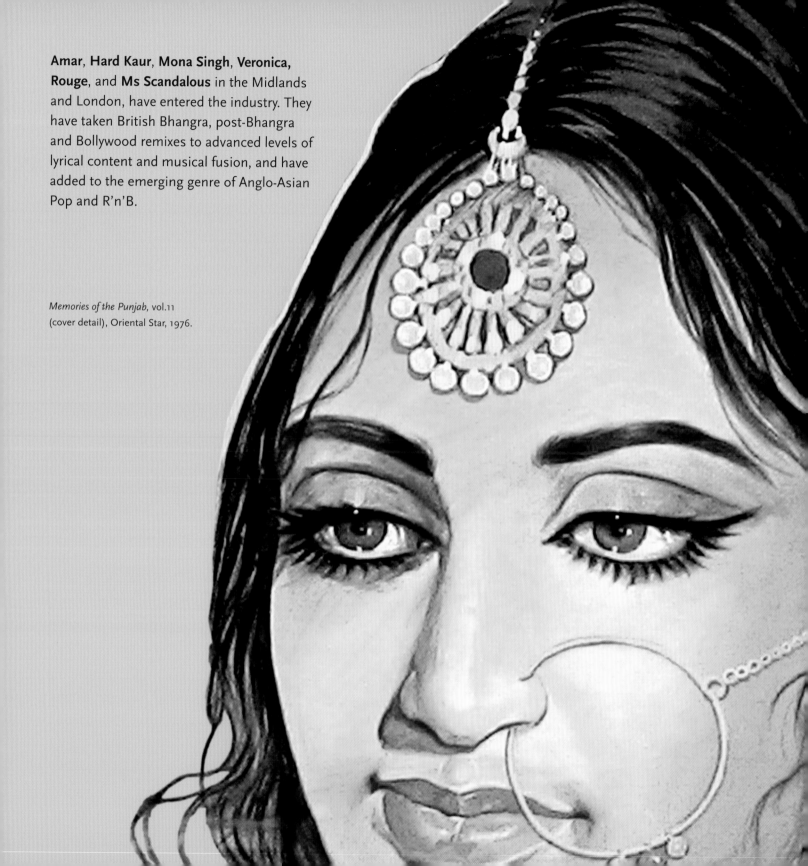

Amar, **Hard Kaur**, **Mona Singh**, **Veronica**, **Rouge**, and **Ms Scandalous** in the Midlands and London, have entered the industry. They have taken British Bhangra, post-Bhangra and Bollywood remixes to advanced levels of lyrical content and musical fusion, and have added to the emerging genre of Anglo-Asian Pop and R'n'B.

Memories of the Punjab, vol.11 (cover detail), Oriental Star, 1976.

Hard Kaur often sings about men's sexual impropriety towards women, but also allows the women protagonists in her songs agency of their own choosing to accept the male advances on offer or to reject them outright in the heart and mind games that can follow.

Hard Kaur (Taran Kaur Dhillon) for instance has adopted US-based Rap styles and Hip-Hop with Bhangra influences to make incisive comments on the racist aspects of British society from policing in the inner cities to racist attacks. Furthermore, she has regularly developed her stage image. Early on in her career she donned slack urban attire with dark glasses to create a no-nonsense demeanour for herself. More recently, she has fused urban chic styles with South Asian dress codes. She is also outspoken in her lyrics, often commenting on sexual politics. Hard Kaur often sings about men's sexual impropriety towards women, but also allows the women in her songs to accept the male advances on offer or to reject them outright in the heart and mind games that can follow. Such female artists defy simple and easy classifications of Asian femininity as exotic and passive.

The emergence and development of newer female artists, prepared to challenge stereotypes, need to be assessed in terms of the opportunities available to women to sustain themselves as artists and to produce themselves anew. Anupreeta and Sameera ended the interviews on a positive yet cautious note, being well aware of the force of sexism and the need to overcome it:

Right: Birmingham-based artist, Hard Kaur.

RD: What do you think needs to be done in order for women to have greater access and control into, and in, the Bhangra music industry?

Anupreeta: The industry needs to accept that women can also produce good music. They have completely ignored and bypassed them and they have rejected them by thinking 'women and music, no it can't happen'. I don't know whether the record companies are doing enough for them as well. They need to be launched in the right way, their image needs to be portrayed in the right way. So to some extent the record companies could be doing a bit more in terms of publicity with the radio stations and media. I must admit there are some presenters on the radio who have really supported women artists in a nice way, and there are female presenters who have actually promoted and supported women in the right way. I don't know whether there is a simple answer that could make changes overnight. It needs a lot of commitment, a lot of work and giving away some power which I don't think sections of the Bhangra industry are ready to do, because giving away something is considered as a loss. It should be about sharing power and access and what they have.

Sameera: For women to do well in the industry or in any sphere, they should be encouraged by friends, families and their wider social circles... I hope to break through into the mainstream. I have sung in English and would like a chance to get wider appeal. I would ultimately like to sing in Bollywood, I hope I find the right contact. If I was a man I think I could just fly over, but as a woman it isn't as easy.

Also of importance are the female DJs **Radical Sista** and **Ritu** who respectively played and promoted UK Bhangra alongside other music at numerous club events throughout the UK. DJ **Rekha** from New York has also been important, playing Bhangra and other tunes on either side of the Atlantic during her appearances at international clubs. DJs Ritu and Rekha have also been playing South Asian music at club venues for South Asian gays and lesbians.

Women artists, then, continue to 'make noise' and contribute to British Bhangra music as it moves forward in the new millennium.

1   *Ghidda* follows beats and rhythms performed at various paces. The female dancers enact verses called 'Bolis' (couplets). These represent a wide variety of subjects – from family arguments to political affairs. The rhythm of the dance depends not only on the use of the drum beat but also on the rhythm and claps of the dancers.

2   I have argued elsewhere how selected British Bhangra tracks which contain dubious lyrics in relation to dominate caste and gender groups can be contested by its audiences (see Dudrah 2002a).

3   The interview extracts used in this chapter were conducted as part of a larger PhD thesis research during 1997 and 1998. The interview material, although now a decade old, is still revealing of some aspects of the workings of the British Bhangra music industry in relation to the role and input of its women artists; some of the issues are still relevant today. For a more detailed account of this research see Dudrah 2001; and 2002. The three artists quoted here, who were interviewed by the author and gave freely of their time and contributed insights, are:

Mr Ninder Johal, Managing Director of Nachural Records; as well as Manager, and tabla player of the Birmingham-based British Bhangra band Achanak. Nachural Records, formed in 1991, is one of the few remaining record labels in the Bhangra industry and is still signing new acts, as it did with Tigerstyle in 2005. Ninder has been involved in the playing and production of Bhangra music since 1988.

Mrs Anupreeta Kumar, female vocalist of numerous Hindi remix albums and British Bhangra tracks, has worked solo and in duets with male singers from the British Bhangra industry. Having been classically trained as a singer in India in her teenage years, Anupreeta became involved in the British Bhangra music industry and Hindi remix scene in 1990 after singing at a friend's party and being overwhelmed by the response she received. From then, she began singing live with a number of Hindi bands in the North West of England, performing all over the country before moving into the recording studios. During her seven years of performances and production, conducted in her 'spare time', Anupreeta has recorded seven albums and has others awaiting development. In 1995 at the Asian Pop Awards held in Birmingham, Anupreeta was awarded the 'Favourite Female Newcomer'. Anupreeta has also been the female singer of the band Tarang (Melody). Tarang consisted of four other band members, all male, who together performed a wide range of South Asian popular music in addition to British Bhangra.

Miss Sameera Singh came to England when she was five-years-old in the late 60s. She started singing as a hobby during her childhood and was trained by her mother, 'to sing and be in tune', who had been formally trained with a degree in classical music. Sameera sang in public at weddings and parties and at Asian festivals up and down the country. In 1992 at the Nottingham Asian Arts Festival, Sameera was approached and then signed by Nachural Records. Since 1992 she has sung and worked on 13 albums, solo or duet, with other male artists. She has also recorded with Apache Indian on his album *Wild East* (Sunset Records, Birmingham, 1998) on the track *Lovin*. This track was immensely popular and was released as a single. Sameera has also worked full-time as a primary school teacher in Northamptonshire.

4   Male artists will almost always dominate the top ten sales of music albums in the British Asian music press. See for example music chart listings on the internet.

Bhangra daytimer, The Hummingbird, Birmingham, 1987.

6 Bhangra's DJ culture

Boy Chana

The Boy Chana offers a personal account of the rise and importance of the British Asian DJ in the story of British Bhangra music.

'So you want to be a DJ!?' exclaim your parents, as you park your bass bins in their living room and set up your Technics SL1200's in your bedroom to practice your mixing techniques for your next gig. In the 80s, British Asian parents may have frowned upon their children becoming DJs. However, times have changed rapidly regarding the perception of the Asian DJ as a profession – one that has mushroomed both on the Asian wedding circuit and the club scene. Asian disco roadshows have grown as businesses, and the bedroom and club DJ in the 00s is now the most wanted producer of British Bhangra music, taking over from the bands since the heyday of live music.

A successful DJ plays and mixes the songs that people want to hear. Bhangra DJs mix records on the deck and some have mastered the art of combining rhythms and beats from the latest chart hits around the world with Bhangra music. The Disc Jockey is considered just as important as the band that headlines a live gig, and even at Asian weddings where a live band has been hired, a DJ can often be seen backing them up. Sadly, the live band scene has been in decline since the mid-90s.

There is a great song lyric from the Hip-Hop artists De La Soul's song, *Magic Number*, 'everybody wants to be a DJ,

DJs are the best!'. In this spirit, the boy next door has thrown away his electric guitar and *dholaks* (Indian drum) to pick up a mixer and a pair of turntables. Sections of young British Asian men and women are turning to DJing creating a mini business for themselves, mainly on the weekends; driving up and down the country for weddings and attending to thousands of students all across the land wanting bass in their face. Similar to Reggae sound systems, the roadshow culture in Bhangra music was also defined in the mid-to-late 80s. Maverick roadshow DJ and record label boss, **Mick St Clair**, explains how he got into the business:

I started DJing in the early 70s at my local youth club as my family had migrated to the Midlands from the Punjab. My musical up-bringing of Punjabi folk came from my parents which they brought along with them when I was four. Listening to Mohammed Sadiq, Ranjit Kaur and Kuldip Manak at home was nothing new but as a teenager I became aware of music around me at school and youth clubs of Albright and Tividale Comprehensive. I blended the two genres together so I played music of my parents and the new sounds of 60s and 70s chart music like Reggae. Not coming from a musical family, it was an outlet for me to represent and push my own traditions and reach out to other Asian families in the area. My first gig in 1976 was as a supporting act for the group the Saathis (Friends) with Jarnail Dosanjh in the Blue Gates Pub in Smethwick (Birmingham).

Gursharan Chana (AKA Boy Chana).

**BALLY
SAGOO ON
THE MIX**

1. JUGNI—
**MALKIT SINGH
"GOLDEN STAR" (UK)** (8.33)
2. JEWEL—
**USTAD NUSRAT FATEH
ALI KHAN** (7.32)

Written by: 1. M. Singh arr. B. Sagoo,
2. Trad. arr. B. Sagoo

Copyright Control

℗ 1991 Oriental Star

This compilation
℗ 1993 Island Records Ltd
The copyright in this sound
recording is owned by
Oriental Star and is exclusively
licensed to Island Records Ltd
in the UK

LC 0407

BIEM STEMRA

SIDE TWO
BALLY 1-B
33⅓ RPM
STEREO

ISLAND

For Promo Only—
Not For Resale

...ING, REPRODUCTION, HIRING, LENDING, PUBLIC PERFORMANCE AND BROADCASTING PROHIBITED

In the British Asian market, DJs rose to fame via the daytime gigs of the 80s. The early DJs were often 'your mates' who liked to listen to music and had a great collection. They began to cater for an audience and carried bags full of tapes covering the DJ booth. Along with these tapes there was the odd LP (long play record) of say a **Gurdas Maan** album, but that was most probably stolen from an older brother's collection!

In the early 80s the radio presenters were not to be seen, only heard, and were more likely to play the finer music of popular Indian cinema and folk Punjabi music. One team that stood out was the **Aaj/Kal** (Today/Tomorrow) crew of **BBC Radio Derby** in the mid-to-late 80s. They were Kash, Surinder, Poli, Pepsi, Nicky and the female Bobbi – the first radio DJs to compare large events and promote artists in the way that the BBC Asian Network are doing today. The events of the 1980s were where these DJs came to champion music for the second generation British Asians wanting a voice and visible popular culture within a changing post-war Britain. It was shows like Aaj/Kal which were tuned into via FM and medium wave as youth as far afield as Derby, Wolverhampton, Birmingham, Coventry, and Leicester, down to Northampton, tuned in on a Friday night. The show proved essential listening as it relayed information of what was going on in the British Bhangra scene as well as playing the latest music. It quickly established itself as the first point of call for all producers, bands and music listeners across large parts of England.

104·5 VHF **Radio Derby** 1116 kHz

1.Satvinder Rana 2.Mobeen Kosar 3.Poli Tank
4.Nicky Baines 5.Kashmir Sahota 6.Yasmin Kosar

The inspiration for starting DJing was my family. I picked up a few LPs that were in our collection at parties and as soon as I earned pocket money, I started to collect more LPs. I soon set up a small rig with some mates and I got my first break when I was 17. My parents thought it was some fly-by-night thing, but I had a flash of inspiration to take DJing to another level and emulate some of the Reggae sound systems we were hearing in the area. By the age of 21 I was DJing and also promoting at some of the biggest clubs across London and it was always great to DJ in the Midlands. We cut our first record, a single called *Jugga* with the band **Dosti** (Friendship), and then the *Extra Hot* album collection took off where me and by brother fused Bollywood with Bhangra and the current trends of dance and club music of the time.

Aaj/Kal, BBC Radio Derby, 1988.
Below: DJ San-j Sanj.

DJ San-j Sanj

San-j Sanj, from London, was one of a handful of DJs who bought a certain vibe with him wherever he performed. He certainly knew how to connect with his audience wherever he was playing from south London to the Midlands, using mix and scratch techniques. For me to get a ticket to see San-j Sanj and his brother Amit of **X-Ecutive** was like getting gold dust. San-j Sanj now fronts his own show on Club Asia radio which broadcasts across London and on the internet. As he explains his in-roads into DJing:

San-j Sanj has earned himself a well deserved reputation based on his years of hard work as a DJ. Most DJs will recount the times spent lugging huge speakers around and fumbling, trying to find out what lead goes where, and what song to put on next. The spread of Asian roadshows, boosted by the wedding circuit, has grown considerably. If a poll was to be taken of DJs nationwide, you would always forget one, as someone will be quick to tell you that 'a friend of a friend has just started up two weeks ago'. Professional set-ups, like that of Mick St Clair, have nurtured a handful of new

REGINE'S

Åcid Bhangra

DJ'S césare, amit & sanjay
Tuesday's 10·30-3·30 £4
Comedy Store
Leicester Sq

recruits over the past 20 years who have gone on to successfully DJ on the club circuit. San-j Sanj also helped to support **Ameet Chana** (actor in the hit film *Bend It Like Beckham* and DJ on the BBC Asian Network) and **Khusty** (promoter) for his later *Extra Hot* remixes and club nights at Limelights in London.

DJs are developing across the country. The rise of record labels like **Untouchables** and **Vips**, from Scotland, has bought the North in line with the popularity and success of DJs in the South and the Midlands in terms of music distribution. As San-J Sanj explains:

> The Asian kids just wanted to hear good Bhangra music...I loved cutting House and Bhangra mixes in the Midlands while our sets in the South were influenced by the R'n'B sound.

Live sound systems are where it is currently at. Some of the biggest names like **Sting** in London, **Nu-Sounds** from Wolverhampton, and **Delsonic** of Yorkshire each cost over £1,000 to hire, and carry technical gear and indoor fireworks worth over £30K to

The early DJs were often 'your mates' who liked to listen to music and had a great collection. They carried bags full of tapes covering the DJ booth, along with the odd LP that was most probably stolen from an older brother's collection.

cater for all venues. The contemporary DJs are creating a musical performance consisting not only of records and CDs but pyrotechnics too.

From vinyl to CDs: DJs now

In the late 90s, record companies started to limit the amount of vinyl being produced due to the rise and popularity of CDs. DJs like San-j Sanj started to press their own records to play at the weekly club nights. **Bally Sagoo** and more recently **Zeus**, who were original bedroom DJs, mixed Bhangra and Bollywood to the latest music trends and revitalised an industry which was shouting out for something new. Also during this period, the bootleg mixes of Bhangra and Bollywood tracks started to be sold through the array of retail outlets, some even behind the fruit and veg counter of your local corner shop.

Today the scene for live bands at gigs is virtually non-existent and bedroom producers are increasingly cropping up. DJs are the cheaper alternative to live bands; as such the DJ has become the most wanted asset for a gig promoter. Some DJs are also using the latest computer software to produce music for new and young singers. Often the singers have no bands and thus rely on the technical know-how of music production that the DJs can offer.

On the mainstream crossover front, corporations like the BBC in the UK have implemented flagship shows like the DJs **Bobby Friction and Nihal** show on Radio 1. On BBC1Xtra (on the internet and via digital radio in the UK), the **Panjabi Hit Squad** have created a name for themselves playing Bhangra and *desi* (diasporic South Asian) beats, mixed with a multitude of other genres. And as acknowledged in the previous chapter, the female DJs Radical Sista and Ritu have respectively played and promoted UK Bhangra alongside other music at numerous club events throughout the UK. DJ Rekha from the USA has also been important, playing Bhangra and other tunes on either side of the Atlantic during her appearances at international clubs.

So, if you still want to be a DJ then think again. If your answer is 'yes', then check your bank balance and ask a few mates to help you out. Most DJs have taken at least three to four years to establish themselves and to secure some form of a part-time career. In the end, the love of music coupled with good business sense will see you through!

Left: promotional poster for Acid Bhangra club night; X-Ecutive promo logo. Below: Pirate Radio Apna's bedroom studio equipment, 1989.
Overleaf: Aaj/Kal playlist.

SIDE A
45 RPM
CTC1001A

COME FOLLOW ME
APACHE INDIAN

PROD. & MIX. BY
SIMON J. DUGGAL
(THE HOOD)
MASTERED BY
MAURICE
TEL: 021-554 6418

THE RECORDED WORK RESERVED UNAUTHORISED PUBLIC PERFORMANCE BROADCASTING AND COPYING OF THIS RECORD PROHIBITED

W/A	MOVE	POS	TITLE	ARTIST	GOAT 5	DATE	WKN5	HIG 14	WAFE 14
191	■	1	JATTA JMAB —	AZAAD	2	23/8	20	1	3
92	↑	2	BOMB THE TUMBI —	SAFRI BOYS	6	21/6	7*	1	4
92	↓	3	TERE ISHQ NACHAYI —	MALKEET SINGH	3	3/12	13	1	5
91	↓	4	SIGNATURE —	ACHAANAK	5	23/5	31	1	5
0/91	↓	5	ISHK —	SAHOTAS *	1	16/8	14	1	3
91	↓	6	KOHINOOR —	HEERA	2	14/8	23	1	2
0/91	↓	7	POWERED UP —	SHAKTEE ✱	3	11/8	18	1	3
91	↓	8	SAQI —	SAQI ✱	5	6/12	30	1	1
91	↓	9	DHOL BLASTERS —	WINNIE/SHARON CALLUS	16	13/12	26	1	3
92	↑	10	HIT THAT DHOL —	GEET	12	7/6	9*	1	3
0/91	↓	11	VIBES —	JOHNNY ZEE	6	16/8	13	1	3
91	↓	12	INNOVATION —	ANAAMIKA	5	13/12	12	2	2
91	↓	13	NA DIL MANG VE — ALAAP	18	20/9	17	1	1
92	↓	14	EXTRA POWER — TSB/Calder Star	18	27/1	13	2	2
91	↓	15	AROUND THE WORLD — PREMI	12	20/1	16	1	1
91	↓	16	FLOWER IN THE WIND — SANGEEM	11	22/1	24	2	1
92	↓	17	NEVER MIND THE DHOLAKS — SAT RANG	8	1/5	12	3	1
92	↓	18	ALIVE + KICKING — SHAAN	17	6/3	12	3	1
91	↓	19	TOUCH OF CLASS — AKAASH	10	23/8	12	4	1
91	↓	20	DANCE FORCE/NITAN DAKITOR — APHOKA	5	16/10	11	5	1

~Kal National Chart

Nicky, Satvinder, Bobby

ACC.	S.R.	RUN (LOWEST)	D² WA D² L WO. GL. WL SL G M B C
OUTLET	POS.		SEQUENCE.
6.35	300	19	2,2,1,1,2,3,3,5,2,5,7,8,9,10,10,14,11,16 [13]
2.28	298	7*	6,3,1,1,1,1,3* still in
6.00	297	13	3,1,1,1,1,1,4,7,8,8,12,12,19
9.03	278	19	5,1,1,1,1,1,2,6,7,9,6,8,11,14,12,12,6,6,10,
5.57	258	14	*1,3,3,3,6,4,4,8,3,7,7,17,16.
9.82	255	23	2,1,1,2,2,3,5,4,4,9,9,13,11,14,12,11,11,18,18,20,20,9,19
6.16	246	18	4,5,4,4,3,2,6,5,6,4,4,6,9,7,13,12,17
6.76	237	17	5,3,1,6,7,5,7,2,6,9,3,10,5,3,13,9,9,
7.25	216	26	16,7,3,6,3,2,1,1,1,2,3,3,2,6,7,13,13,14,10,6,12,13,15,12,11,16
3.11	196	9*	12,1,1,1,2,4,2,3,4* still in
8.53	186	13	6,6,7,8,9,10,11,11,11,12,20,20
8.91	176	8	5,2,2,3,8,10,9,11,16,16,13,12
9.35	146	17	18,1,2,2,2,3,4,6,9,8,8,8,12,20,19,18,19
7.15	141	13	18,7,4,5,4,2,2,7,8,6,3,11,16
8.06	138	16	12,1,2,2,3,5,5,7,6,9,13,10,10,12,18,17
9.37	125	12	11,5,3,4,4,5,4,4,5,3,2,8,
7.63	125	11	5,4,5,6,4,5,7,8,13,11,15.
1.30	71	12	13,3,5,8,9,9,11,14,11,14,17,18
12.25	64	12	10,9,11,4,9,13,14/16,14,13,16,18
13.01	60	11	5,7,8,11,11,16,14,18,20,15

7 The beat goes on: British Bhangra now

Rajinder Dudrah

The British Bhangra music industry is undergoing diversification, taking up the call for new South Asian music genres as album production and performance niches. British Bhangra has also come to influence different styles of Bhangra music the world over such as Canadian Bhangra and, interestingly, traditional folk Bhangra in the Punjab too. Folk Bhangra, in particular, has become more technologically upbeat since it was introduced to its diasporic cousin. With the popularity and influence of British Bhangra pulsating in India, musical exchanges have taken place between legendary artists of the Punjab and with bands in Britain. For example, male folk artists such as Gurdas Maan and Hans Raj Hans, whose careers span over 20 years respectively, have been regularly touring Britain with much success, and British bands have been well-received in India. Moreover, the racy UK Bhangra beat which struck a chord with folk artists in the Punjab, in turn, caught the imagination of listeners throughout India via its national distribution outlets. Folk Bhangra's meeting with the British Bhangra beat soon caught on and became translated into Bollywood film soundtracks since the late 90s. Recent Bollywood-Bhangra examples include songs from the films *Kal Ho Naa Ho* (Tomorrow May Not Be, dir. Nikhil Advani, 2003), *Kabhi Alvida Naa Kehna* (Never Say Goodbye,

dir. Karan Johar, 2006), *Namastey London* (Greetings London, dir. Vipul Amrutlal Shah, 2007), and *Jhoom Barabar Jhoom* (Dance Equally Dance, dir. Shaad Ali, 2007).

The diversification of the British Bhangra industry has also led to a number of developments, some more welcomed than others, throughout different sections of the industry. For instance, since the 00s an emerging preference for DJs on the wedding circuit is superseding the hiring of live bands. DJs can be hired much cheaper for a three to four-hour party with the most popular DJs incorporating a *dhol* player, live mixing, and an indoor firework show. This has brought to the fore an affordable culture of music entertainment and dancing, predominantly orchestrated by young men whose creative flair and technical wizardry has brought them into the limelight with British Bhangra enthusiasts. However, this also means that bands increasingly have to compete with monetary scales that weigh in favour of the DJs. As such, the opportunities for live performances of British Bhangra bands remain to be seen.

More annoyingly, the late 90s and early 00s also witnessed the cheap and hurried production of British Bhangra and Bollywood

Flyposters promoting the new wave of British Asian artists, 2004. Below: BBC Radio 1 and Asian Network DJ, Bobby Friction.

remix albums by a few opportunists. These were being spewed out in several numbers each month by a few young male remixers who were more interested in making a 'fast buck' than developing artists or producing new and innovative sounds. In some extreme cases the quick technological production of Bhangra and Bollywood remixed tracks is done without permission of the original artists or bands.

Such albums often go unchallenged by the Asian record companies due to the large legal bills involved in bringing about redress. By a way of response, the frustration of keen South Asian music producers and lovers was aptly captured in an article by one of *Eastern Eye's* music commentators, Wicked Miah [pseudonym]. As the headline caption read in his humorous and bold report:

> We let our pet rat Chakk de Patel free at the record shops to sniff out some of the new releases. He returned with a fistful of monkey's plop and put forward the question: What is this rubbish? (*Eastern Eye* 6/3/1998:8)

Far from the cry of a gullible audience buying into anything and everything that the machination end of a music industry might throw at it, British Bhangra music listeners and critics are informing themselves of the 'not-so-good music' which finds it way into music stores vying for consumers' cash. **Ninder Johal** from **Nachural Records** in Birmingham also concurred with this view, as he put it:

> Album sales were higher in the early 90s as a lot of people were into the Bhangra scene and buying different tapes seeing what's on the market. Now [late 90s] the figures aren't as high as they were for say an average artist. Well-known artists obviously continue to sell in big numbers. The market and audiences have matured, nothing is instantly sellable. They know that there's some real crap being churned out so they only go for what they like.[1]

Tigerstyle

With Bhangra audiences in Britain, on the whole, more critical as to what they are purchasing and listening to, it is hoped that the few crass opportunists will be weeded out, or learn to respect audience taste and produce more pleasurable music. Meanwhile, music producers like Ninder Johal, of Nachural Records, are busy looking to develop the British Bhangra market overseas, partly contributing to the growth of the genre of World Music in recent years. As Ninder revealed in a magazine interview contemplating the future of British Bhangra after its heyday heights:

> We have had all the limelight in the UK over the last ten years. You can only take a market so far until that market becomes stagnant. Bhangra was big business for us in the 80s now it helps to pay the bills. But the big deals are elsewhere to be found. We have since '95 been looking at the market overseas and that doesn't just mean in India, which would have been the first port of call. There is such a large market for Bhangra outside the UK that we have been so busy that we have had to delay releasing records for the UK market. We have just set up deals in France, Italy, Holland, and we already have deals in Japan and the Far East. (Boy Chana 1998:35)

With the live band music scene having declined since the heydays, British Bhangra beats and lyrics have been taken up by the wider Asian music scene in Britain and fused aplenty. British Asian artists like Jay Sean have crossed over into the mainstream international pop charts in the 00s and often lace their tracks with Bhangra. **Adil Ray**, a radio presenter on the BBC Asian Network, recalling developments since his Bhangra revelling days as a teenager in the 80s says:

> ...we've got artists like, **Rishi Rich**, **Juggy D**, **Jay Sean**, and **Raghav**. So it was part of, you know, that era coming through. Bhangra music in my time really moved on from the live stuff, which we can complain about as it's sad to see some of the live bands go. But it's really more DJ-based, studio production-based, more Dance music-based. And I think that you're less likely to go to a Bhangra gig now. What you'll go to is an Asian gig that'll actually be 70% playing R'n'B, you know, and Rishi Rich and Jay Sean fits in somewhere in the middle. Then you've got Juggy D who's kind of still full-on playing some of the Punjabi stuff. Sadly, the whole live band thing where you'll go to The Dome in the early days and you'd see four to five live bands playing one after the other, those days have gone.

Even in its latest moments of fusion, then, British Bhangra is still developing further and assists in renewing the genre of British Asian music. In fact for some remix artists it is crucial to how they have developed their brand and musical identity. As Adil Ray surmises on a few of the key Bhangra players in the UK of late:

> I think the people who really come to mind are **Tigerstyle**, for me. You've got two very devout Sikh Punjabi's from Glasgow, who know their Bhangra music more than anybody. I mean they absolutely know their stuff. They're young, they're the right generation. If you listen to some of their earlier

In recent years, the larger mainstream chains such as HMV and Virgin have been selling Bhangra compilation albums as part of their World Music and Desi Beatz categories.

albums they were ground-breaking then. What they do and what they've done is, they will still play the traditional stuff, but they will effortlessly fuse it into Dancehall or Hip-Hop. And the beauty of them is that they both know the genres of music. So they know Bhangra and they know Hip-Hop. And it all works together, it sounds great. And they can perform live. They recently did BBC Electric Proms where they performed live with a four-piece classical quartet. Then they had Gunjan and Raja sing with them as well and Desi from the **Mentor Kollektiv**. And I think that is really interesting, really clever. We've still got the traditional Punjabi music. We've still got the element of live and it's still taking it forward. I love what **Swami's** done in recent years. For a while he was taking it more Dance-based, but now he's getting back into live stuff with a rural Rock feel – the *Desi Rock* track. Clearly I love what bands like **Achanak** are doing, because musically they haven't necessarily moved it on too much. They have tightened up their production, which is good, but they are really important, because they probably have a bigger appeal outside of the UK than they have inside the UK. They'll often go to Europe, Denmark, Germany and play to sell-out gigs of majority white young Europeans, which I find quite interesting.

Others in the Bhangra music industry are optimistic that the live band Bhangra days are not totally over and could well be reinvigorated through a concerted effort by all. As **Gurcharan Mall** of **The Dhol Blasters** in Birmingham put it:

Asian Dub Foundation logotype. Below: The Kray Twins.

Ok, you know for like the word to go around the changes need to happen. Ok, people are using Drum and Bass and everything, that's good. We want our Punjabi folk instruments to get involved too. The only thing that discourages me is when kids are using, or senior artists...ok, kids you can't blame them simply because they are limited to money, but when big artists they start using sample work, they are putting decent good musicians out of work. That's a little bit naughty. Like I always say, kids go into Drum and Bass, go into this, go into that. But please, please, please know your roots, so what ever you've built on top it'll be much stronger...Bhangra is here to stay. Fads will keep on coming in, different things will come in. Live bands would start, but this is good as well because it's tightening the bands up as well. Say well look ok, we've got the DJs to compete against, what do we need to do? They need to book a bigger PA system and do a lot of other things like what the DJs are doing. So keep the price sensible, so people who do want to book them, and, I strongly feel that Bhangra will never die out. It's going stronger and stronger, and live bands can come back. And even the DJs they are happy, they don't criticize about live bands. All they say, well as long as we are booking too...They (the bands) need to make their own *kismet* (destiny) by working hard. If you work hard then people will book you.

Bhangra in Birmingham and beyond: now and in the future

British Bhangra no longer suffers from the invisibility of previous decades. The success of Birmingham's **Bally Sagoo**, who started his music career in the 80s remixing British Bhangra tracks, is fitting testimony to the enduring work of British Asian artists. Sagoo now heads **Ishq Records** in Bordesley Green in Birmingham, signing up-and-coming talent and distributing their work around the world. He encourages his artists to be innovative and bring together different people to enjoy the music. As he states on his website: 'I am Asian, loud and proud, but I'm also British. I hope to have captured all those influences in our music, for people all around the world to relate to. For me, our music represents bringing different worlds together and uniting them as one' (www.ishqrecords.com).

Birmingham-based BBC Asian Network has been influential in promoting British Bhangra music on the airwaves. Below: Members of BBC1Xtra's Panjabi Hit Squad.

British Asian artists like Jay Sean have crossed over into the mainstream international pop charts and often lace their tracks with British Bhangra.

British Bhangra artists **Malkit Singh**, and producer-turned-singer **Sukshinder Shinda**, also from Birmingham, remain popular, attracting large audiences and listeners among South Asians worldwide.

The music has also made inroads into mainstream popular culture through the fusion of different styles and aesthetics found in the work of, amongst others, **Apache Indian**, **Asian Dub Foundation**, **Gurinder Chadha**, **Bobby Friction and Nihal**, and BBC1Xtra's **Panjabi Hit Squad**.

Radio stations have always been crucial for disseminating Asian music in Britain, a position strengthened by the broadcasting of the BBC's Birmingham-produced **Asian Network** throughout Britain (available on 1458 MW in the Midlands, via Digital Audio Radio and online). The Asian Network continues to champion the history and developments of Bhangra music.

Asian music and video shops on the Soho Road in Handsworth are good and friendly places to shop for the latest and back catalogue of British Bhangra releases. Alum Rock Road, Smethwick High Street (also in Birmingham), and similar streets around Asian areas of settlement in the UK have equivalent stores. In recent years, the larger mainstream chains such as HMV and Virgin have been selling Bhangra compilation albums as part of their World Music and Desi Beatz categories.

More recently, a new generation of British Asian singers, dancers and music producers have emerged throughout the country, drawing inspiration from the early pioneering Bhangra artists from Birmingham and London. The **RDB** brothers from Yorkshire and **DJ Vips** from Scotland can be set alongside the **DIP** boys, **Dalvinder Singh**, and DJs **Koka Krazy**, **Jet Jagpal**, **Mukhtar Sahota**, **Dr Zeus**, **Aman Hayer** and the **Kray Twins**, all from the Midlands.

Below: Shin and MC Metz. Opposite: Coventry's Panjabi MC had a international hit with *Mundian To Ke Bach Ke* (Beware of the Boys) which sampled the bassline from the TV show *Knight Rider*.

This shows that British Bhangra is here to stay, with Birmingham undoubtedly a focal point. Equally important in terms of the place of British Bhangra production is the city of Coventry, 17 miles south of Birmingham, which continues to be influential. As lyricist Bal Sidhu confirms:

> A lot of good music was created in Coventry and even now we get a lot of the big artists recording in Coventry. **Johnny Zee** is from Coventry, **Stereo Nation**, **Panjabi MC**, **Anaamika**, **Baldev Mastana** is from here now and **Salinder Pardesi** is doing it from here. **Planet Studios** are the most famous studio in the pre-*Pump Up The Bhangra* days and **Shinda** and **Jazzy B** have worked in Planet. It's a very popular studio and it's run by gore (white Brits). I remember sitting with **Malkit Singh's** wife listening to him while he did his vocals... He used to do the music in Bombay and come and do the vocals here and Planet is the place. It was quite interactive.

Birmingham's and the wider West Midlands region's production and distribution companies continue to circulate the music around the world, its artists – old and new – performing locally and globally. The lives of British Asians will keep on providing scripts to work with in the songs, music and dancing of British Bhangra.

1 Extract of interview taken from Dudrah (2002:221).

Bibliography

The Style of the Overseas Woman – book of lyrics by Balwinder Singh Sidhu.

Works cited

Banerji, Sabita and Gerd Baumann (1990) 'Bhangra 1984–88: Fusion and Professionalization in a genre of South Asian Dance Music' in Paul Oliver ed. *Black Music in Britain*. Milton Keynes: Open University Press. pp.137–152.

Baumann, Gerd (1990) 'The Re-Invention of Bhangra. Social Change and Aesthetic Shifts in a Punjabi Music in Britain', *World of Music*, vol.32, no.2, pp.81–95.

Boy Chana (1998) 'Who said Bhangra is dead?' in *Generation*. Birmingham: Birmingham Post & Mail Publications, pp.34–35.

Dudrah, Rajinder (2001) 'British South Asian Identities and the Popular Cultures of British Bhangra Music, Bollywood Films, and Zee TV in Birmingham', Unpublished PhD Thesis, Department of Cultural Studies and Sociology, School of Social Sciences, University of Birmingham.

Dudrah, Rajinder (2002) 'Cultural Production in the British Bhangra Music Industry: Music-making, Locality, and Gender', *International Journal of Punjab Studies*, vol.9, no.2, pp.219–251.

Dudrah, Rajinder (2002a) 'Drum 'n' Dhol: British Bhangra Music and Diasporic South Asian Identity Formation', *European Journal of Cultural Studies*, vol.5, no.3, pp.363–383.

Huq, Rupa (1996) 'Asian Kool? Bhangra and Beyond' in Sanjay Sharma et. al; *Dis-Orienting Rhythms: The Politics of the New Asian Dance Music*, London, Zed Books.

Sharma, Sanjay; John Hutnyk and Ashwani Sharma eds. (1996) *Dis-Orienting Rhythms: The Politics of the New Asian Dance Music*. London: Zed Books.

Further reading

Bennet, Andrew (1997) 'Bhangra in Newcastle: Music, Ethnic Identity and the Role of Local Knowledge, *Innovation*, vol.10, no.1, pp.107–116.

Din, Ikhlaq and Cedric Cullingford (2004) 'Boyzone and Bhangra: The Place of Popular and Minority Cultures', *Race Ethnicity and Education*, vol.7, no.3, pp.307–320.

Dudrah, Rajinder (2002) 'British Bhangra Music and the Battle of Britpop: South Asian Cultural Identity and Cultural Politics in Urban Britain', *Migration: A European Journal of International Migration and Ethnic Relations*, vol.39/40/41, pp.173–193.

Gopinath, G. (1995) 'Bombay, UK, Yuba City: Bhangra Music and the Engendering of Diaspora', *Diaspora*, vol.4, no.3, pp.303–321.

Huq, Rupa (2003) 'From the Margins to Mainstream? Representations of British Asian Youth Musical Cultural Expression from Bhangra to Asian Underground Music', *Young*, vol.11, no.1, pp.29–48.

Kalra, Virinder (2000) 'Vilayeti Rhythms: Beyond Bhangra's Emblematic Status to a Translation of Lyrical Texts', *Theory, Culture and Society*, vol.17, no.3, pp.80–102.

Maira, Sunaina (1998) 'Desis Reprazent: Bhangra Remix and Hip-Hop in New York City', *Postcolonial Studies*, vol.1, no.3, pp.357–370.

Varma, Sandeep K. (2005) 'Quantum Bhangra: Bhangra Music and Identity in the South Asian Diaspora', *LIMINA: A Journal of Historical and Cultural Studies*, vol.11, pp.17–27.

Useful websites

www.achanak.co.uk
www.apnaorg.com/music/punjab
www.asianclubguide.com
www.asiandubfoundation.com
www.asianrhythm.com
www.bbc.co.uk/asiannetwork
www.bhangraomega.com
www.dcs-band.com
www.desiclub.com
www.desitunes4u.com
www.ishqrecords.com
www.nachnach.com
www.nachural.co.uk
www.osa.co.uk
www.pmcrecords.com
www.realbhangra.com
www.shaanti.co.uk
www.ukbhangra.com
www.viprecords.co.uk
www.xlnc-theband.co.uk

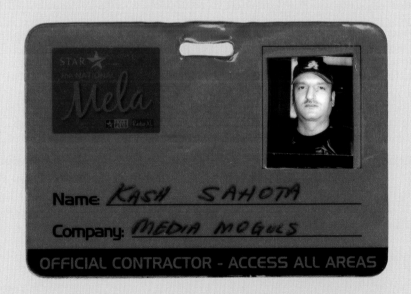

Kash Sahota's backstage pass for Star TV's National Mela.

Index

Below: Bhangra album chart, 1991.

Overleaf: Malkit Singh and his brother Harvinder Singh during a recording session at Dep International Studios, Birmingham.

Back page: Punjabi Geet, vol.1 (cover detail).

The Legendary
joe bloggs
Asian Pop Awards 1991
369 High Street, West Bromwich, West Midlands B70 9QL

ALBUM RELEASES FOR 1991
----

1. NON STOP BOLIAN - BALBIR BOBBY.
2. CHALLA CHANDI DA - ARISHMA RELEASE.
3. ARE YOU FEELING - SAHOTAS.
4. BHANGRA MANAK DHA - KULDIP MANAK.
5. DISCO VICH TUMBA - DILSHAD AKHTER.
6. JULLUNDARON PAAR - BALBIR BOBBY.
7. EXTRA HOT 3
8. REFLECTIONS - BALWINDER SAFRI.
9. GARM A GARM REMIX.
10. BEAT THE RAP - DAL.
11. GAL SUN JA - MAKLIT SINGH.
12. HAYE OIYE - MANGAL SINGH.
13. AR TUT DI - HANS RAJ HANS.
14. MOVIE OVER INDIA - APACHE INDIAN.
15. HOUSE OF SHAH - MICK ST CLAIR.
16. NEW EXCUSE - SABRAS.
17. DEOR DA VIAH - PREMI WEDDING SONGS.
18. VAISAKHI - PANKAJ UDHAS.
19. SWEET POWER - TARLOCHAN S BILGA.
20. POWERED UP - SHAKTEE.
21. COME FOLLOW ME/MOVIE - APACHE INDIAN.
22. JAZZ - JAZZ.
23. GOLDEN STAR RAGA MUFFIN MIX - BALLY SAGOO.
24. EXTRA HOT 4 REMIX.
25. CHILLIN - GEET MEGABAND.
26. VIBES - JOHNNEY ZEE.
27. OVER THE TOP - PREMI.
28. JEWEL - NASRUT/BALLY SAGOO REMIX.
29. HASAN DE MALKO - SARDOOL SIKANDER.
30. POWER PACK - REMIX MULTITONE.
31. SONE DA PARANDA - SHANU.
32. ISHK - SAHOTAS.
33. WA WA - SUKHDEV S SANGHA.
34. KHUSHIAN - APNA SANGEET.
35. SUBEDAAR - G. MANN.
37. MITRAN DHA KHOO - ASHOKA.
38. BHANGRA BOMBSHELL - RED ROSE.
39. LAL GAGRI - BALBIR BOBBY.
40. RAP ON - BALI BALI GOOD - BALI.

41. mehdi sagua dee.

81

To you
with Love!!